COUTURE SEWING

The Couture Cardigan Jacket

Sewing secrets from a Chanel collector

CLAIRE B. SHAEFFER

The Taunton Press
Inspiration for hands-on living®

The Taunton Press, Inc.
63 South Main Street
PO Box 5506
Newtown, CT 06470-5506
e-mail: tp@taunton.com

Executive Editor: Shawna Mullen
Editor: Katherine Marrone
Copy editor: Betty Christiansen
Indexer: Catherine Goddard
Jacket/Cover design: Stacy Wakefield Forte
Interior design: Stacy Wakefield Forte
Layout: Cathy Cassidy
Illustrators: Steve Buchanan and Christine Erikson
Photographer (All jackets and jacket details): Liam Goodman
Stylist: Angela Hastings
Video stills/Step-by-step process photos: Gary Junken

The following names/manufacturers appearing in *Couture Sewing:
The Couture Cardigan Jacket* are trademarks: Vogue Patterns®

Library of Congress Cataloging-in-Publication Data

Shaeffer, Claire B.
Couture sewing: the couture cardigan jacket : sewing secrets from a
Chanel collector / Claire B. Shaeffer.
     pages cm
  Includes index.
 ISBN 978-1-60085-955-7 (paperback)
1. Jackets. 2. Tailoring (Women's) 3. Chanel, Coco, 1883-1971. I.
Title. II. Title: Couture cardigan jacket.
 TT535.S33 2013
 646.4'5--dc23

This book is in honor of the 2013 Chanel centennial, and is dedicated to the late Gabrielle (Coco) Chanel, who opened her shop in Deauville a hundred years ago.

ACKNOWLEDGMENTS

Although the author is credited with the success of a book, every book involves many people with expertise in a variety of areas. This is especially true when the project includes a DVD. It gives me great pleasure to thank all those who have contributed to *Couture Sewing: The Couture Cardigan Jacket.*

I would especially like to thank Louise Passey, Linda Homan, Esli Navarro, and Sarah Castro, who made the many samples for the DVD; my editor, Kathy Marrone; and photographer Liam Goodman. I would also like to thank Sarah Benson, Lynn Cook, Margaret Duffy, Nancy Erickson, Fred Dennis, Lourdes Font, Anne Kendall, the late Charles Kleibacker, Harold Koda, Joy Landeira, Julie Le, Timothy Long, Phyllis Magidson, Hazel Mathys, McCall Pattern Co., Bob Purcell, the late Elizabeth Rhodes, Dennita Sewell, and Carole and Leslie Walker, as well as the members of VintageFashionGuild .org and my students, who have provided information, encouragement, and inspiration.

I particularly appreciate the support of Amann-Mettler, Apple Annie, Bernina USA, Britex Fabrics, Linton Tweeds, Redfern Enter-prises and Eurosteam Irons, Sawyer Brook Fabrics, and Superior Threads for providing materials, supplies, and equipment for the project.

Many people at The Taunton Press helped to make a challenging project successful.

I would especially like to thank my editor, Shawna Mullen, the video team—Judy Neukam (technical editor), Victoria North (producer), and Gary Junken (videographer)—and the book team—Renee Neiger (in-house editor), Erin Guinta (photo editor), Angela Hastings (stylist), Kimberly Adis (art director), Nora Fuentes (edit production), and Cari Delahanty (video editor).

Thanks also to the following institutions and their staffs: the Art Institute of Chicago; Museum of Fine Arts, Boston; Brooklyn Museum; Chicago History Museum; Costume Institute of the Metropolitan Museum of Art; Edward C. Blum Design Laboratory at the Fashion Institute of Technology; Fashion Institute of Design and Merchandising, Los Angeles; Special Collections at the Fashion Institute of Technology; Fine Arts Museum of San Francisco; the Irene Lewisohn Costume Reference Library; Kent State University Museum; Lake Blackshear Regional Library, Americus, Georgia; Los Angeles County Museum of Art; Museum of the City of New York; Phoenix Art Museum; Powerhouse Museum, Sydney, Australia; Royal Ontario Museum; History Museum at the Smithsonian Institution; Stephens College; Texas Fashion Collection at the University of North Texas; and the Victoria and Albert Museum.

Lastly, I would like to thank my husband, Charlie Shaeffer Jr., M.D., for his continued support and encouragement.

CONTENTS

This jacket is from the 1970s and is as light as a feather. The novelty weave fabric is backed with beige silk, and the fuchsia tie matches the companion blouse.

INTRODUCTION

I began the research for this book more than
30 years ago. Along the way, I've examined more
than 300 Chanel designs—mostly suits and coats—
in 17 museum and private collections. During that
time I've amassed a personal collection of Chanel
designs, which includes more than 75 couture pieces,
a variety of ready-to-wear designs, and many copies.
The House of Chanel guards its workroom and
archives very strictly, and my several requests to visit
them in order to learn their construction techniques
have been turned down. But that hasn't deterred
me from trying to figure them out on my own.
So I focused on what I know—traditional haute
couture construction and how it has been applied to
garments in my collection, how other designers use
similar techniques, and what I have learned through
my experience teaching others.

From 1967, this classic jacket has a stand collar which has been
shaped to fit the neck edge. The jacket is subtly shaped with
princess seams. The quilting on each side of the narrow cream
stripes is almost invisible.

In the end, I had enough data for several books and had to limit the focus of this one and the accompanying DVD to the cardigan jacket. The techniques that I describe are my techniques. They may or may not be the same as those used in the Chanel ateliers, but they will enable you to create a fabulous and unique couture-quality cardigan jacket.

It goes without saying that the classic cardigan jacket is timeless and has a place in every woman's wardrobe, no matter what her age. This enduring design has been popular for more than 50 years and is unmatched for its appeal. With simple yet sophisticated lines, it lends itself to being fabricated in a great variety of fabrics and trims, giving it a fabulous versatility that can change its look from sporty to elegant. Wear it with jeans to the market or with an evening skirt to the opera . . . you'll always look elegant.

From 1970, this go-anywhere Chanel jacket is simply trimmed with a turn-down collar, flaps, and lion's head buttons. The edges are piped with dyed-to-match wool knit and lined with a plain weave silk.

CHAPTER ONE

Getting Started

From the mid-1960s, this evening jacket is fabricated in silk and metallic brocade. The trim is crocheted with silver thread to make an insertion. There are no visible fasteners.

DESIGN AND MATERIALS

Have you always dreamed of owning a classic cardigan design? Most of us have. Well, now your dream can come true by making your own! It's easier than you think, especially if you enjoy hand sewing. But first comes one of the really exciting parts of making the jacket—planning it. Study the designs of Chanel, Yves Saint Laurent, Escada, Adolfo, and Davidow for inspiration. Then select a great cardigan jacket pattern and make a muslin test garment (also called a toile). Next, choose a fabulous fabric and experiment with various trims. The choices are as limitless as your imagination.

"If a fashion isn't taken up and worn by everybody, then it is not a fashion but an eccentricity, a fancy dress."

—COCO CHANEL, VOGUE, 1954

FABRICS, PATTERN, AND MUSLIN

Most often, the classic cardigan jacket is thought of as a tweed or plaid garment, but that is not the rule. It can be made in almost any fabric and for any occasion, from sporty to evening. The choice of fabric will dictate whether the jacket is quilted by hand or machine, or maybe not at all. It will also influence whether or not trims are added, and if they are, whether or not they are simple or ornate.

1. The more elaborate the fabric is, the less you want to add to it. Therefore, laces, metallic brocades, and embellished taffetas such as these should not be machine-quilted. If quilting is desired on these fabrics, it should be done by hand, inconspicuously. Trims are often simple, such as a solid ribbon, and should be kept to a minimum, or not used at all.

2. This group of fabrics would make up beautifully in a classic style and would be perfect with machine quilting. Because these fabrics are dark and muted, the style of trim will greatly influence the final look of the jacket; boldly braided metallic or beaded trim and buttons give it a glamorous evening air, while subtle, flatter edgings make it more sporty.

3. The most traditional choices for the cardigan jacket are nubby tweeds and plaids in soft pastels or neutral shades such as these. Most are made from wool or wool blends, but you can also find cotton tweeds, such as the blue fabric in the center. In the 1960s, machine quilting was a status symbol because the copies were rarely quilted.

4. Since lining and trim are important elements for the classic cardigan, be aware that finding the perfect match may prove to be a challenge. This neutral tweed was such a case. Finding a matching lining fabric was time-consuming and expensive. The silk charmeuse fabric that was eventually found was as costly as the wool fashion fabric. The lesson is that you have to think ahead about the entire project, not just the shell fabric.

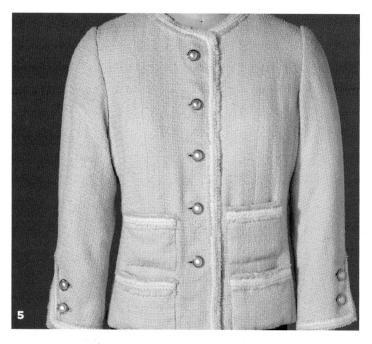

5. When selecting your pattern, look for one with princess seams, a jewel neckline, a two- or three-piece sleeve with a working vent, and patch pockets. Vogue Patterns'® V8804 from Claire Shaeffer's Custom Couture Collection is the one that is used for all the examples shown here. Before cutting into your fashion fabric, you should always make a muslin toile or test garment to refine the fit and practice any new sewing techniques.

NOTE Find lots of trim ideas in the Appendix, beginning on p. 123.

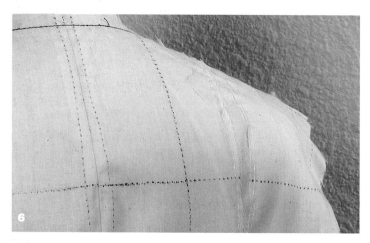

6. When fitting the toile, establish the buttonhole locations and sleeve lengths, as these details are sometimes completed on individual garment sections early in the assembly process. With all the fitting and details perfected on the toile, you can concentrate on assembling the garment with confidence.

GUIDELINES FOR SUCCESS

- Read all directions before cutting your fabric. Some of the techniques and the order of assembly are quite different from traditional home-sewing methods.
- Make a muslin toile to fine-tune the fit before cutting the fashion fabric.
- Don't eliminate any thread tracings. They are crucial guidelines for assembly.

- Make or purchase shoulder pads at the outset and insert them for every fitting.
- Don't skip on basting.
- Press, press, press. When tailoring, it's not uncommon to spend more time pressing than sewing.
- Practice, practice, practice. Perfect your skills for individual elements before applying them to the garment itself.
- Preshrink all materials appropriately for the fiber content at the outset.

COUTURE COLLECTION

This stunning Chanel jacket is fabricated in a novelty open-weave stripe. The solid-color collar, hem, and sleeve bands were created by stitching tucks in the fabric to remove the beige stripes—a clever manipulation of fabric to create trim.

ALL ABOUT TRIMS

Braid trim, sometimes called gimp, is one of the most common edgings for a classic cardigan jacket, but there are many other options. Flat or embellished ribbons are probably the next most popular trim, with piping coming in third. Why not be as creative as Chanel herself, who was known to be very innovative and sometimes used the wrong side of the fashion fabric or coordinating blouse fabric for trim? Here are some ideas.

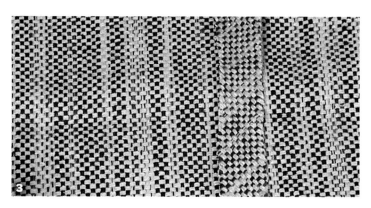

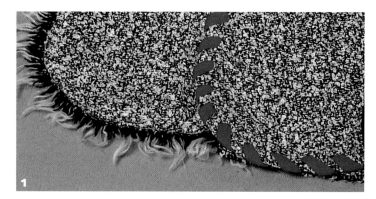

1. Not all trims are stitched to the top of the garment. The feathery trim on the left is applied to the wrong side, and the one on the right is soft ribbon whipstitched over the edge.

2. You can also make your own braid. Here are four ideas that were made as samples for the brown tweed fabric in the background. From left to right: Black gimp sandwiched between gold piping; fashion fabric wrapped with wide black grosgrain ribbon; two colors of narrow grosgrain ribbon butted together and stitched, with a narrow gimp layered on top; black gimp layered on brown ribbon.

3. This unusual multithread woven cotton suiting gave inspiration to a multilayered trim. The base is a strip of bias-cut self-fabric.

4. On top of the bias strip, a grosgrain ribbon was added, then a narrow white/blue gimp. To give it a pop of color, you could swap out the blue ribbon for a bright red ribbon. Don't be afraid to try unusual color combinations. You may be surprised at the outcome.

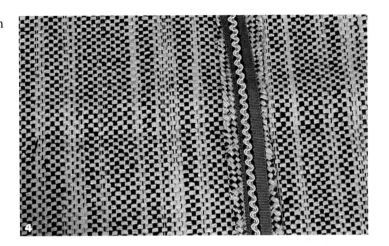

FRINGE

Fringe is still one of the most popular trims. It can be made with self-fabric or a matching fabric such as the solid basket-weave fabric shown here.

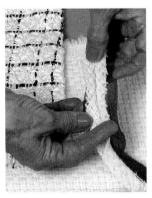

To make a fringe, the fabric is sewn to a piece of chiffon or soft organza, and the chiffon is hand sewn to the underside of the garment so that only the fringe shows.

Cut bias strips of fabric twice the width of the desired fringe. Stitch the bias strip to a bias chiffon strip through the center. The chiffon can be the same width or slightly wider than the bias strip.

Fold the fashion fabric in one direction and the chiffon in the other. Zigzag-stitch over the center seam to hold the trim flat.

Use a tapestry needle to unravel the threads and create the fringe. If necessary, trim the fringe to an even length. Apply the trim to the jacket shell from the underside.

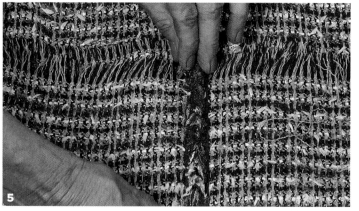

5. With a loosely woven novelty tweed such as this one, several yarns can be unraveled and crocheted into a single chain. If the colors blend into the fashion fabric too closely, place the thread chain on a colored grosgrain ribbon to frame the crocheted chain. The result is unique and can be stunning.

NOTE When looking at trims, hold them vertically against the fabric because that's the way they will be seen when the jacket is worn.

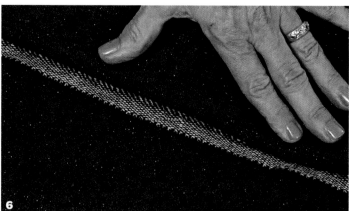

6. The selvage edges of fabric are a good source of trim. It's a good idea to save the selvage edges from all your fabrics. There are lots of ways to use them as trim, or you can turn them into piping. Organize your trimmed selvages in plastic bags by color for easy retrieval.

7. Here's an over-the-top idea. Use feathers as trim. Sew them loosely by hand so that they are easy to remove for cleaning or to change at a later date.

8. For the jacket in this book, many options were tried before settling on the final choice. Different shades of gimp were layered on a variety of ribbons and between piping. See p. 134 for the final choice.

FLAT PIPING

The lining is another good source for trims. By extending the lining past the edge of the fabric to form a narrow decorative edging, you can create a flat piping.

At middle right is a sample. Since it is not corded, the edge is flatter and softer than a corded piping. It has a subtle, sophisticated look.

On the underside (bottom right), the lining is smooth and flat with pickstitches so the piping maintains an even width. Make a sample before you begin to be sure you like the look. If you prefer a corded piping, you can add a cord before finishing the lining.

This beautiful jacket is shaped inconspicuously with princess seams at the edges of the gold stripes.

CUTTING AND MARKING

The cutting and marking process is very different from that of home sewing. A muslin or paper with seam allowances is positioned on the fabric matching the grainlines, then the seamlines are thread-traced onto the fabric. The couture method of construction is to match the seamlines, not the cut edges; therefore, seam allowances can be any width and are often trimmed after the garment sections are stitched together. Because of this, seamline markings are crucial and must be accurate. All markings are with thread, as opposed to chalk, so that you can see them on both sides of the fabric and they will not disappear with handling.

"I've read that Chanel believed there was nothing prettier than a well-made toile."

—Claire Shaeffer

NOTE The method used for this jacket is quite different because the jacket is quilted. Each section and its lining begin as rectangles. Then the individual fabric sections are quilted to the lining sections before they are sewn together.

THREAD-MARKING THE FABRIC

Cut rectangles of fabric a few inches wider and longer than each pattern piece. These rectangles are easier to quilt than garment shapes and allow for the possibility of shrinkage, which can be caused by the quilting.

1. Mark the grainline on the fabric with thread. Next, make a catchstitch (X) to mark the top of the rectangle. This is very important if your fabric has a nap or one-way design, so that you always know which direction to place your pattern piece. It will also indicate the right side of the fabric, which can be hard to distinguish from the wrong side, especially on a tweed.

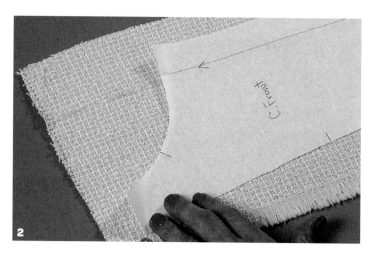

2. Position the pattern piece on the fabric matching the grainline on the pattern to the grainline on the fabric, and pin in place. Thread-trace around the pattern piece. Reminder: The pattern pieces do not have seam allowances, so thread-trace right at the edges of the pattern.

3. In addition to the seamlines, thread-mark all construction symbols (notches, circles, triangles, and squares). Notice that the corners are marked very precisely, which is important for exact matching during assembly. The construction symbols are marked with short basting stitches across the seamline. These symbols can be notches, circles, triangles, or squares on the pattern.

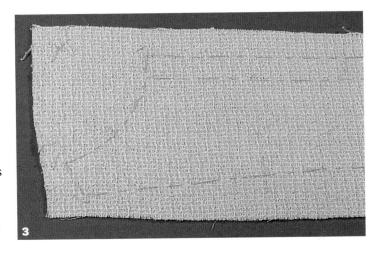

4. For a nice, sharp corner, put the needle into the fabric right at the end of the seamline and bring it out about ½ in. beyond. Then insert the needle ½ in. before the beginning of the next seamline, bringing it out exactly at the corner. Continue thread-marking the seamline. Repeat at all corners.

NOTE Blue thread is used for the thread tracing on the samples so you can see it easily. When sewing the garment, always use white basting thread for the thread tracing.

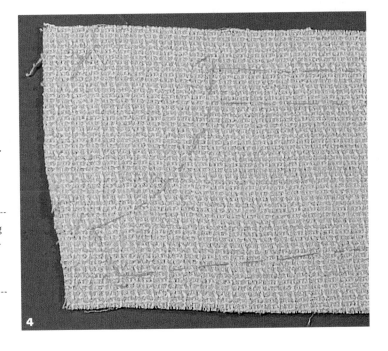

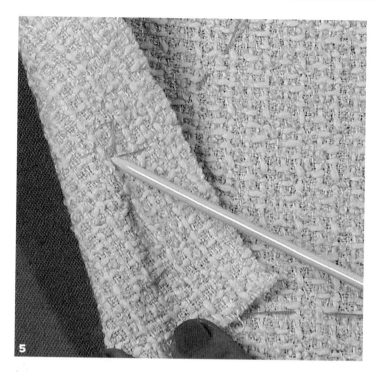

5. On the wrong side, the corner point is also precisely marked, which makes it very easy to match corner points from the right side and wrong side during construction.

6. Clip the corner threads so that they will be easier to remove later. Mark the remaining sections for the jacket body in the same manner.

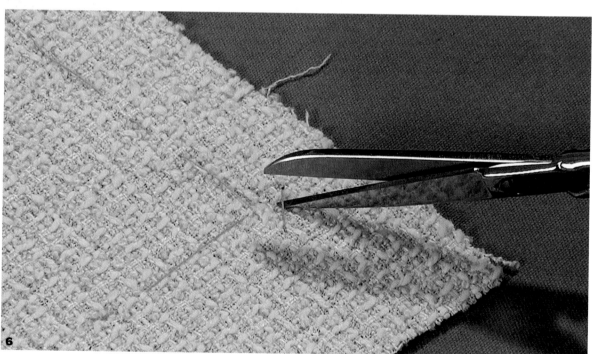

COUTURE COLLECTION

This beautiful Chanel jacket from 1967 is made in a plaid fabric, which requires precise cutting and marking to keep the vertical order of stripes (thick, thin, thick, thin) going around the body in order. Note that the sleeves have been carefully matched to the jacket body.

CHAPTER TWO

Constructing the Jacket

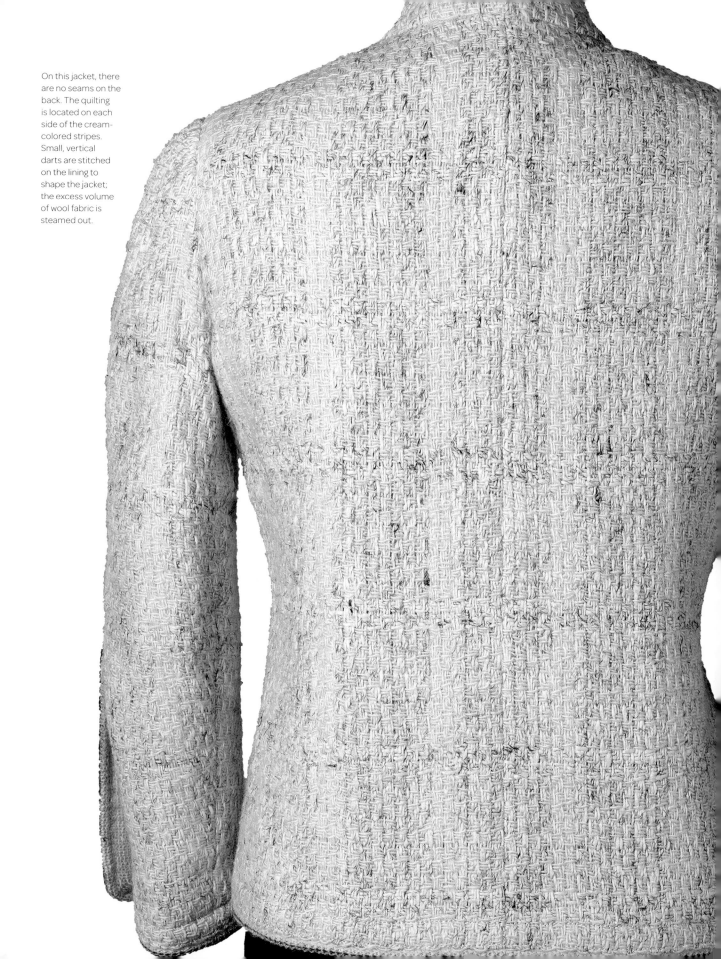

On this jacket, there are no seams on the back. The quilting is located on each side of the cream-colored stripes. Small, vertical darts are stitched on the lining to shape the jacket; the excess volume of wool fabric is steamed out.

QUILTING THE JACKET

An important element of many Chanel jackets is the quilting. Since the quilting was rarely used on the copies, it is a status symbol. But this is not your typical quilting, since there is no batting between the layers. It is simply fashion fabric quilted to lining. On some garments, the stitches blend in with the fabric and are nearly invisible; on others, they are very obvious. The quilting helps to maintain the structure and shape of lightweight, loosely woven wool tweed or bouclé fabrics without traditional interfacings and tailoring techniques. When worn, the jacket feels light and airy, soft and luxurious, almost like a comfortable sweater.

Coco Chanel famously said . . . "Elegance means a thing's as beautiful on the wrong side as on the right."

WHERE AND HOW TO QUILT

Quilting is the first step when constructing this classic cardigan. For this method, rectangles of fabric and lining are cut for each section, then they are quilted together before they are assembled. Since the fashion fabric is quilted to the lining—except for the front, which is quilted to interfacing—the order of construction is very different from the typical tailored jacket.

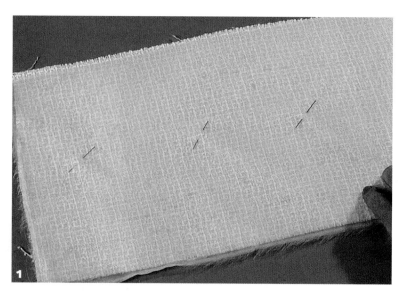

1. Cut rectangles of the lining fabric —in this sample, silk charmeuse—to match each thread-traced garment section. Cut a rectangle of organza to match the thread-traced front piece; this will be the interfacing. Start by pinning the organza to the front piece with wrong sides together, aligning the edges. Baste in place with a row of diagonal stitches on the grainline.

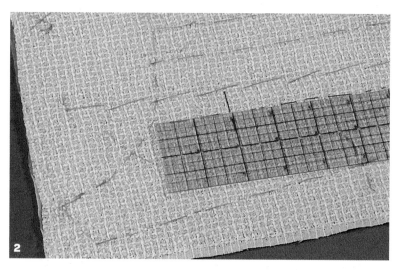

2. Use pins to mark the quilting line on the front piece. On this jacket, the quilting line is 2 in. from the side-front seam. Place a pin at the top of the quilting row, 2 in. below the neckline.

TIP When the fabric is loosely woven, use additional quilting rows.

3. Place another pin at the bottom of the quilting row, 2 in. above the hemline. It is important to keep the quilting 1 in. to 2 in. away from the seamlines and hemlines to allow room to turn under the seam and hem allowances during assembly. Proceed to stack the lining and fashion fabric rectangles, wrong sides together, for the remaining body sections. Pin-mark the quilting rows following the same guidelines.

4. Before basting the quilting rows, compare the front and side-front pieces. Look at the spacing of the quilting rows to the seamline and see how they relate to each other. If necessary, make adjustments to the quilting rows now to avoid ripping out later.

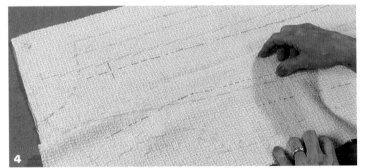

5. Replace the pins marking the quilting lines with thread tracing (red thread). Then sew a row of diagonal basting over the quilting line (purple thread). This will keep the layers from shifting during machine quilting.

NOTE I used colored threads so they can be seen easily. I like basting thread, which has no finish and breaks easily for easy removal.

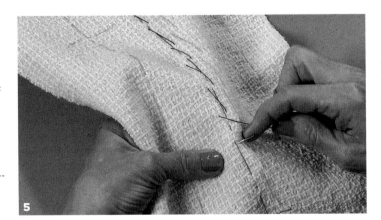

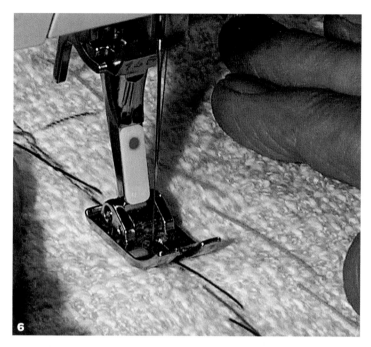

6. With the right side up, machine-stitch next to the thread-marked quilting line. Use cotton thread in the needle and bobbin, and set the stitch length for 4 mm, or six stitches per inch. Stitch precisely to the ends of the marking, and leave long thread tails. On some Chanel jackets, the quilting is done with silk buttonhole twist in the needle, the bobbin, or both.

NOTE Contrast thread is used for the machine stitching so it is easier to see. When quilting your garment, use matching thread.

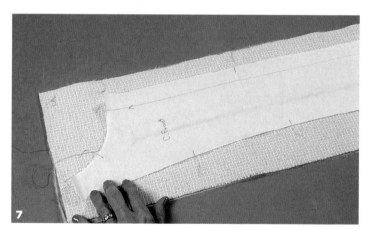

7. Before proceeding, lay the original front pattern piece on the fabric to see if the quilting has caused it to shrink. If it has, thread-trace new seamlines. Do this after each section is quilted.

TIP If you have to adjust the seamline due to shrinkage, don't remove the original thread tracing. Just remark on the new seamline with a different color thread.

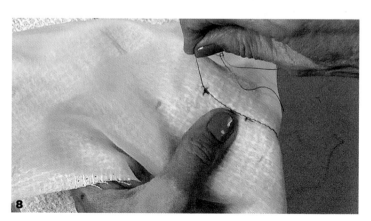

8. To secure the quilting stitches, pull the thread tails to the wrong side of the front. Give them a gentle tug and knot.

9. Remove the basting threads and thread markings that relate to quilting on the front sections. Do not remove other thread markings. Notice that the quilting stitches are almost invisible because they were done with matching thread. The next step is to stabilize the front edge and shape the bust area.

NOTE This quilting technique will be used for the remaining sections of the jacket body.

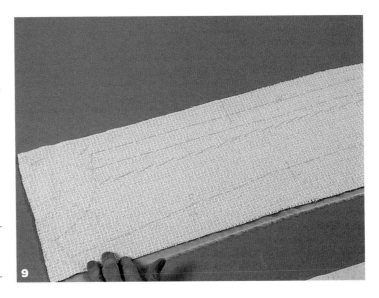

COUTURE COLLECTION

Since the pockets on many suits have no interfacing, they sag; and some are even cut with a curve at the opening to achieve this look. Black yarn whipstitched over the edge adds a distinctive touch to this Chanel jacket from 1964.

From the mid-1970s, this classic jacket in wool doublecloth has a small notched collar. The trim is flat silk braid, hand sewn invisibly to the edges.

STABILIZING AND SHAPING

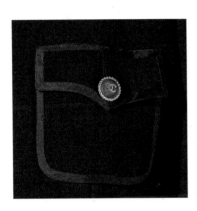

The inside of a couture jacket holds many secrets. Hidden between the layers of fabric and lining are a variety of invisible details that can help an edge hang perfectly straight or shape two-dimensional fabric to fit the three-dimensional contours of the body. Shrinking, stretching, and stabilizing work together to give a garment its final fit. Mysterious as they may seem, they are essential to the jacket's construction, and are easy to learn.

Chanel is often quoted as saying . . . "It's no good if a thing's only pretty as long as it's buttoned up. No woman will want to be imprisoned in that."

HOW TO STAY THE FRONT EDGE

Adding a strip of stay tape along the front edges of the jacket will ensure that they hang perpendicular to the floor when the garment is worn, even if it is unbuttoned.

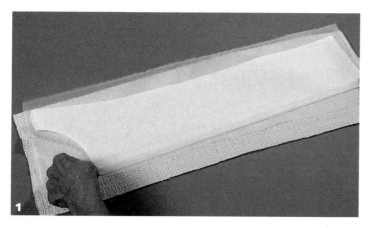

1. For the stay tape, use a piece of selvage from silk organza—the same fabric that is used for the interfacing—or another lightweight silk. Measure the stay against the pattern piece from the seamline at the neck edge to the hemline if you didn't measure for the stay when you fitted the muslin toile. Mark the top and bottom with a pencil.

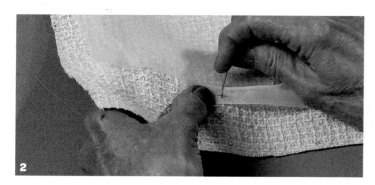

2. Position the stay tape on the wrong side of the jacket, aligning the edge of the tape with the thread tracing at the front edge. Pin one of the marked points on the stay tape to the seamline at the neck. Pin the remaining mark on the stay tape to the hemline.

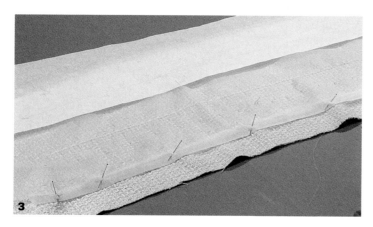

3. Notice that the front edge of the jacket has stretched and is slightly longer than the stay tape and will have to be eased to fit. Use a few pins to hold it in place.

4. Baste the stay tape to the jacket through the center of the tape.

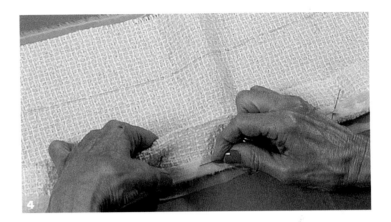

5. Use fell stitches to sew the stay tape to the jacket permanently along the thread-traced line. Stitch carefully so the stitches don't show on the right side of the jacket. Remove the basting stitches from the stay tape.

NOTE Contrast thread is used for this sample so you can see it easily. When sewing the garment, use matching thread.

6. With the wrong side up, fuse narrow strips of interfacing at the location line for each buttonhole. These will stabilize the fabric when the thread buttonholes are made later.

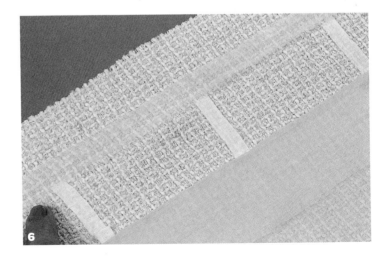

BUST SHAPING AND DART STAY

On the side-front section, the bust shaping is achieved with ease basting, steaming and shrinking, and a bust dart stay. This combination gives lightweight structure to the inside, with invisible shaping on the outside.

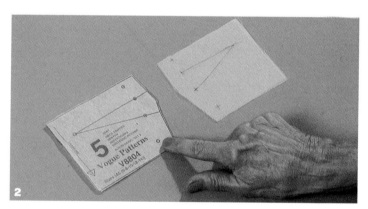

1. Place a row of ease basting on the seamline in the designated bust area. Place another row ⅛ in. away. Pull up the threads and steam out the excess fullness.

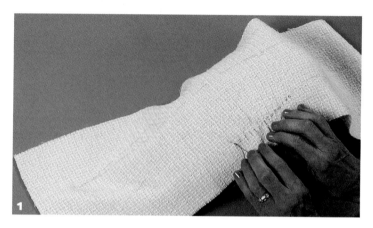

2. Use the dart stay pattern to cut two stays from silk organza. Mark the dart and construction symbols (dots) with pencil as indicated in the photo. Sew the dart closed with short running stitches. Press.

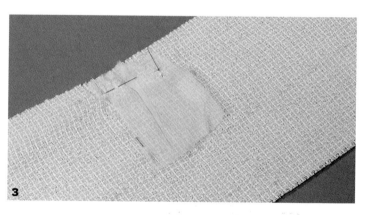

3. With the wrong side up, position the dart stay on the side front in the designated bust area. Adjust the easing on the side front to the dart stay, matching symbols. Pin in place. Baste with diagonal stitches across the top and bottom.

4. Sew the stay in place with running stitches along the seamline, and with catchstitches on the other three sides. Sew carefully so that the stitches don't show through on the right side of the garment. Remove the basting stitches.

NOTE Contrast thread is used for this sample so you can see it easily. When sewing the garment, use matching thread.

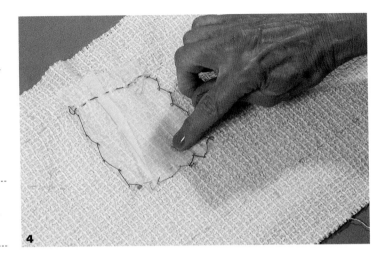

COUTURE COLLECTION

This long wool/mohair plaid Chanel jacket from the late 1960s has no trim because of the boldness of the fabric. To achieve shape without interrupting the stripes of the plaid, the princess seams have been positioned at the outer edge of the vertical gold stripe so they are inconspicuous.

Vintage 1964, this jacket was shaped with heat and moisture for a fit that skims the figure. There is also a small bust dart on the lining.

THE NEW CONSTRUCTION ORDER

Lining is usually the last step in constructing a jacket, but not in this method. For this jacket, the construction order is totally different from other tailoring projects. First, the lining is quilted to the fashion fabric, one section at a time. After quilting, the seams on the fashion fabric are machine-stitched, and the lining seams are closed by hand after the seams are stitched. This is quite different from everything you learned in tailoring, but the results are couture quality.

Chanel loved luxury, and her biographers quote her as saying . . .
"Real luxury to me means having well-made clothes and being able to wear a suit for five years because it still looks good. I adore old suits, things that have been used."

LINING THE SIDE FRONT

The first step is to quilt the lining to the fashion fabric. In the same manner as the front piece, stack the fashion fabric and lining rectangles with wrong sides together, aligning the edges. Baste in place with a row of diagonal stitches along the grainline.

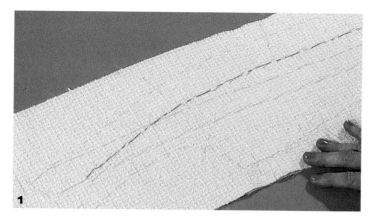

1. This section—the side front—will have two rows of quilting. As on the front piece, the quilting line is marked with thread, and a row of diagonal basting is stitched over it (red threads). (See "Where and How to Quilt" on p. 28 for more details on quilting.) This is the first row of quilting. Notice that it follows the curve of the seamline, not the grainline. Machine-stitch the quilting line and remove the basting threads. The second row of quilting will be marked and stitched later in the process. Pull the thread tails of the quilting stitches in between the lining and fabric. Knot the ends. This will give a clean finish on the inside and out.

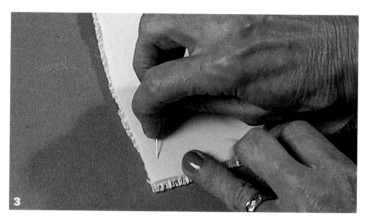

2. With the lining side up, notice that the fashion fabric is shorter than the lining on the side with the dart because of the easing in the dart area.

3. Align the fashion fabric and lining at the top and bottom of this side of the rectangle, and pin in place. The excess fabric will create a bubble in the lining.

4. With the lining side up, place the bust area over a tailor's ham and pin a dart in the lining to remove the bubble. This dart will be on top of the stay dart.

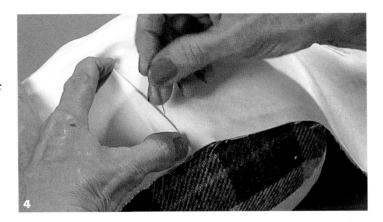

5. Baste the dart in place and remove the pins. Permanently sew the dart closed with fell stitches. Sew carefully, without a knot and without pulling the threads too tightly. Make sure the lining has not been accidentally sewn to the fabric. The layers must remain separate so you can finish the seams later.

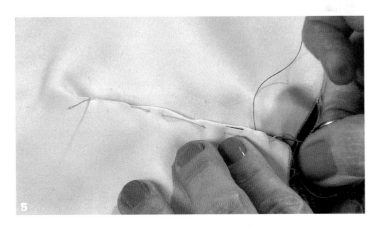

6. Now you can stitch the second row of quilting. Thread-mark the quilting line and diagonally baste over it (purple threads), as you did before. Machine-quilt next to the marked quilting line, tie off the thread tails between the layers, and remove the basting threads. Now the side front is ready to be attached to the front piece.

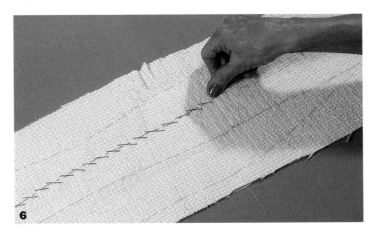

STITCH THE FRONT TO THE SIDE FRONT

The front and side front have been quilted and shaped, and are ready to be assembled. They are still rectangular shapes that will be matched and stitched along the thread-marked seamlines. Here's the way to do it.

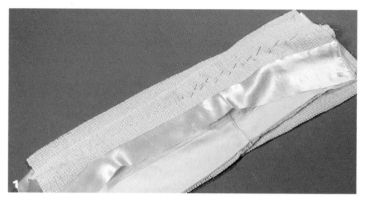

1. Fold the lining out of the way and, with right sides together, pin the front to the side front along the seamline, matching all construction symbols.

2. This is a close-up view to show how to match the seamlines. Insert a pin into one seamline and then directly into the corresponding seamline. Pick up a small bite with the pin to hold the layers together. After pinning, baste the seamline. Remove the pins. Lightly press the basted seamline before stitching. This helps to marry the layers of fabric and keep them from shifting during stitching.

TIP Avoid the temptation to stitch over the pins. Fabric has a tendency to shift during stitching, and basting is easier than ripping out.

---

3. Machine-stitch the seam with a stitch length of 2 mm, or 12 stitches per inch. Begin stitching at the shoulder, which is the point of difficulty. Continue stitching into the hem allowance. Leave long thread tails and knot the ends. Do not back-tack.

4. Remove the basting threads and press the seam flat. Then put it on a seam roll and press the seam open. Press just the stitching line.

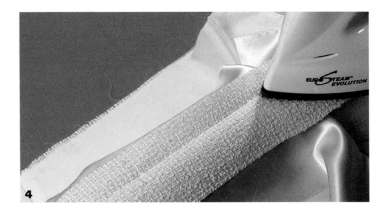

5. With the iron hovering over the seam, give it lots of steam. Then cover it with a clapper and press hard to set the seam. Trim the seam allowances to 1 in. The next step is to finish the lining seams by hand.

NOTE This method for stitching seams together will be used for all garment sections.

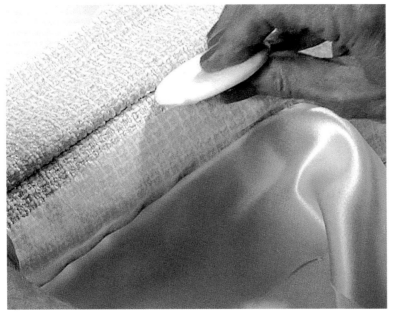

SAVILE ROW TECHNIQUE

This technique is used by some tailors of London's Savile Row, who are frequently considered the world's finest tailors. If the fabric is springy and will not lie flat, use a bar of soap that doesn't have oils in it to help tame the seam. On the wrong side of the fabric, rub the seamline on both sides with a fine line of soap. Press the seam open.

TWO WAYS TO SEW LINING SEAMS

There is often more than one way to complete a task, and finishing the lining seams is no exception. Here are two options; for most seams, you can use the one you like better.

1. Trim the seam allowances of the fashion fabric and lining to about 1 in. The wider seam allowance will press better and drape better than a narrow one. It also allows the option of letting the garment out at a later date.

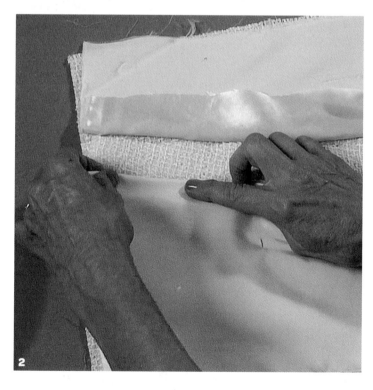

2. For the first technique, fold the lining seam allowance under, matching the folded edge to the garment seamline. Pin in place.

3. Baste the folded lining edge carefully to avoid sewing it to the jacket seam. Fold under the remaining seam allowance in the same manner so the two edges are butted together, or "kissing." Baste the folded lining edge, being careful to avoid sewing it to the jacket seam.

4. Using thread that matches the lining and a long needle, slipstitch the two folded edges together. At the hemline, stitch carefully to avoid sewing the lining to the seam. Further along the seam, it is OK if the slipstitches catch into the seam of the jacket.

TIP When you weave the needle between the two lining folds, the stitches are slanted. This is one of the few times when the threads of the slipstitches can be slanted, since they will show less on these seams than when they are at right angles to the folded edges.

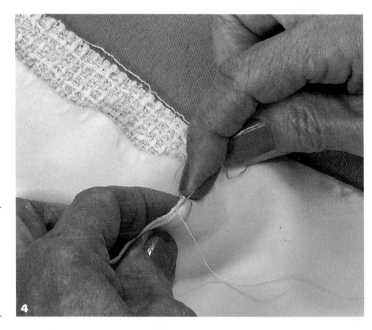

5. The second method for stitching lining seams is a lapped seam. Here, it is being shown on the seam that joins the underarm panel to the side front. As on previous sections, the garment seam has been stitched, pressed, and trimmed.

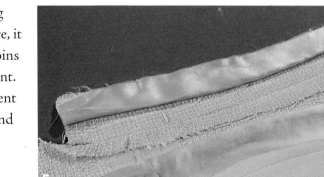

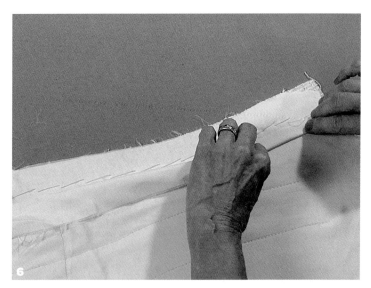

6. Smooth the side-front lining over the garment seam allowances. Sew it permanently with running stitches. Next, turn under the seam allowance on the underarm panel lining.

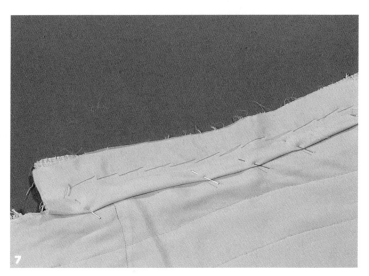

7. Pin the lining along the folded edge, matching the folded edge to the garment seamline. Baste the folded edge of the lining, being careful to avoid sewing it to the jacket seam at the hemline. Use fell stitches to sew the lining seam permanently.

NOTE This method for stitching a lining seam is especially good for an area such as this, where there is a dart. The dart of the lining is not folded, but left flat, so there is less bulk.

COUTURE COLLECTION

Designed by Karl Lagerfeld for Chanel in the late 1980s, this wool and chenille jacket is lined with silk crepe. All of the vertical seams on the lining are lapped as well as the shoulder and armscye, which are lapped and hand sewn.

CHAPTER THREE

Buttonholes

Made with silk buttonhole twist, this beautiful thread buttonhole was embroidered by hand. If you look very carefully, you can see a hint of the bound buttonhole on the facing.

DOUBLE BUTTONHOLES

A distinguishing feature on many Chanel jackets is the buttonholes. They are hand-worked with thread on the shell or fashion fabric, and finished with a faux bound buttonhole on the inside lining or facing fabric. This double buttonhole is used at the front opening, since the thread buttonhole is unattractive on the underside when the facing or lining fabric is a contrast color. A similar buttonhole was used by Charles Frederick Worth when contrast fabrics were used on the jacket and facing.

On jackets, keyhole-shaped buttonholes are generally preferred because they have a larger, rounded end where the button shank will sit when buttoned.

Chanel's designs are precise, and she is quoted as saying . . . "A dress must be made like a watch—if a tiny wheel does not work, make the watch or the dress over."

HANDWORKED BUTTONHOLES

Before making buttonholes on your garment, make a test buttonhole using all the same materials as the "real" buttonholes. Silk buttonhole twist is the best thread choice for handworked buttonholes. Make a sample for each size button being used and check it by inserting the button. If the buttonhole is the least bit tight, it will not wear well. This is also a good time to see if the thread color matches the fabric as planned. If you can't find an exact color match in silk buttonhole twist, try topstitching thread or heavy machine-embroidery thread.

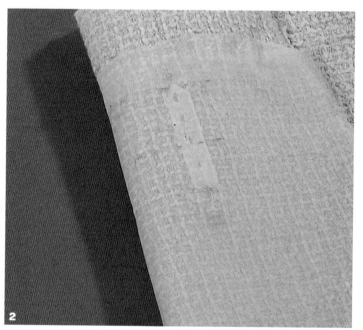

1. Mark the horizontal buttonhole placements with thread. Also thread-mark each end. The buttonholes should extend ⅛ in. past the center-front marking.

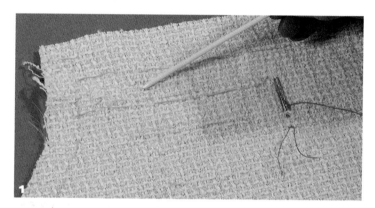

2. To prevent raveling, place a narrow piece of fusible interfacing on the wrong side of the fabric at each buttonhole location if you didn't do this earlier.

TIP Buttonholes look different when viewed horizontally, so pin a sample to a bulletin board and stand back several feet to look at it vertically. You may want a different thread color. Just as musicians need to warm up before a concert, practice your stitches before making the buttonholes on your jacket.

----

3. Using a straight machine stitch set to 1.5 mm (20 stitches per inch), stitch a rectangle around the thread that marks the buttonhole location. The stitching should be a scant ¹⁄₁₆ in. from the thread mark. Begin stitching at the end farthest away from the garment opening, stitch around the buttonhole, and overlap the first few stitches. Use a slightly contrasting thread color, since these stitches will be used as a guide when you make the buttonhole stitches. Remove the buttonhole thread tracings.

4. Cut the buttonhole open, beginning at the center with a small snip, then working out to each end. Clip carefully to avoid cutting the machine stitches. Trim off any raveling threads with the scissors. Seal the raw edges to prevent them from continuing to ravel. You can use a little dab of white glue on a toothpick, wax, or a fray retardant. I prefer glue, because it is easier to control.

NOTE If the buttonhole has a keyhole, the rounded end is positioned nearer the jacket edge.

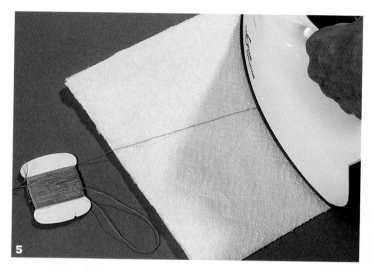

5. Prepare a quantity of thread before beginning to stitch the buttonholes. Unwind several yards of silk buttonhole twist and wax it all at one time. Do not cut the thread off the spool. Draw the thread over a cake of beeswax to coat it. Place paper towels on a pressing board and place the beginning of the strand on top. Cover with a hot iron and pull the thread underneath the iron to melt the wax into the thread.

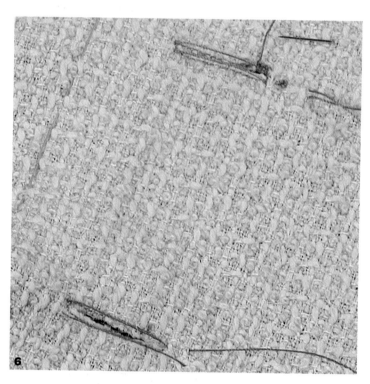

6. Laying a strand of thread on each side of the buttonhole before working the stitches will give it an attractive raised effect, and also give it strength. This is called a corded buttonhole. To do this, insert the needle about ½ in. beyond the end of the buttonhole farthest from the opening, coming out at the beginning of the buttonhole. Do not knot the thread. Insert the needle about ¹⁄₁₆ in. beyond the end of the buttonhole, coming out on the opposite side of the buttonhole. Insert the needle about ¹⁄₁₆ in. beyond the end of the buttonhole, coming out about ½ in. away. Do not knot. Leave long thread tails.

7. Anchor the thread for the buttonhole stitches with a waste knot about ¼ in. from the end of the buttonhole farthest from the jacket opening. The waste knot will be cut off when the buttonhole is finished. Working through the buttonhole opening, insert the needle from the wrong side of the fabric, coming out just beyond the machine stitching. Begin at the end of the buttonhole farthest from the jacket opening.

TIP I usually work from right to left, but it doesn't matter whether you make the stitches from right to left or vice versa as long as you wrap the thread around the needle point in the direction you are going.

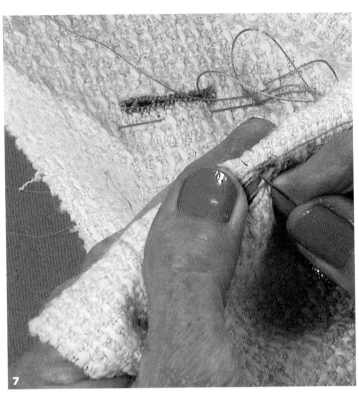

8. While the needle is halfway through the fabric, wrap the thread around the point in a counterclockwise direction if you are right-handed. Pull the needle through the fabric, creating a purl (knot) that encases the raw edge and the strand of cording thread. Continue working from right to left, with stitches very close together. As you work the stitches, use your fingers to adjust and align the purls. Keeping the stitches even in length and spacing is key to a professional-looking buttonhole.

NOTE If the strands of cording thread loosen and wiggle as you work, gently pull on the tail ends to tighten them.

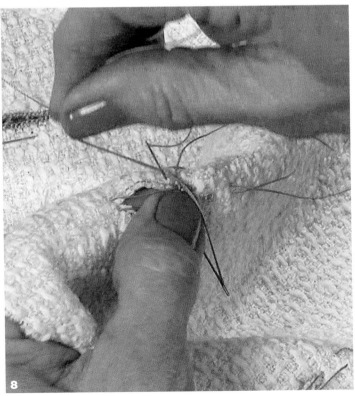

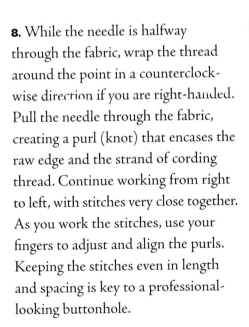

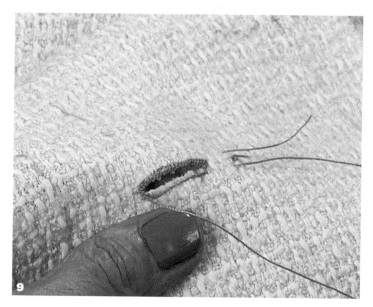

9. At the keyhole end of the buttonhole, fan the stitches attractively in a curve. Continue the buttonhole stitches on the remaining side of the opening.

10. When you reach the starting point, take three stitches to create a short bar at the end. Cut off the waste knot and pull the threads to the wrong side; knot and hide the thread tails between fabric layers. Also bring the tail ends of the stranding thread to the wrong side, and give them a little tug to make sure they are straight and snug under the buttonhole stitches. Tie them together in a knot and hide the ends.

TIP Use your fingers to adjust and align the purls. They can be positioned on top of the fabric or along the opening edges of the buttonhole.

---

11. Cut two welt strips from lining fabric approximately 1 in. longer than the buttonhole and 1 in. wide. Fold the strips in half with right sides together. Pin the welts to the wrong side to cover the buttonhole stitches. Butt the folds together at the center of the opening. Sew them permanently with running stitches. The back of the buttonhole will be covered with lining in chapter 8 (see "How to Finish the Inside of the Buttonhole" on p. 106).

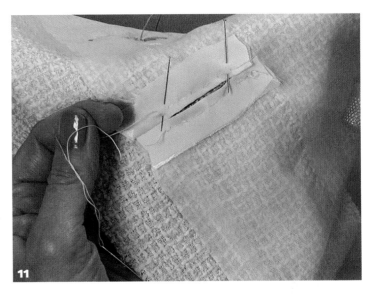

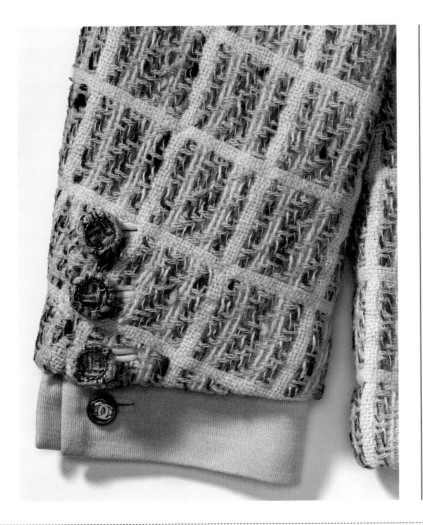

COUTURE COLLECTION

In contrast to most Chanel jackets, the two-piece sleeve on this jacket from the early 1960s features bound buttonholes on the vent made of lining fabric, which is also used for the trim and pocket flaps. The buttonholes on the pocket flaps are made of the fashion fabric. The buttonholes on the faux blouse cuffs are traditional thread buttonholes.

CHAPTER FOUR

Assembling the Sleeves

With the three-piece sleeve, you can achieve a beautiful shape, but you sometimes have to make a sacrifice. Here, the center seam is not matched, but the sleeve front and sleeve back are matched to the body of the jacket.

THE THREE-PIECE SLEEVE

A well-fitted sleeve conforms to the shape of the arm and hangs in a perfect cylinder without ripples and puckers. The frequently used one-piece sleeve will not give you the desired shape for a couture garment. A two-piece sleeve, found in high-quality jackets and coats, allows for better shaping and quality. However, the three-piece sleeve will fit and hang even better; it also positions the sleeve vent so that it is more visible from the front. It is easy to master with a little guidance.

On most Chanel suits, the sleeves are also quilted when the jacket body is quilted. In this chapter, the sleeves will be quilted, hemmed, trimmed, and finished with working vents and handworked buttonholes.

"It has been reported that Chanel believed that sleeves were the quintessential artistry of haute couture."

—Claire Shaeffer

MARKING AND ASSEMBLY

The quilting technique for the sleeve is a modified home-sewing method. The sleeve sections are cut to the pattern shape with seam allowances, as in home sewing, but the order of construction is very different. Read through all directions before beginning to understand the sequence.

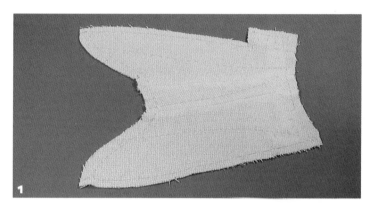

1. The front sleeve, underarm panel, and back sleeve have been stitched together, and the seams have been pressed open. Notice that the grainlines have been thread-marked on all sections. The sleeve front and undersleeve are cut slightly off grain so the sleeve will fit the arm more comfortably.

2. All the seamlines have been thread-traced with ⅝-in. seam allowances, except at the cap and hem, which have 1-in. seam allowances.

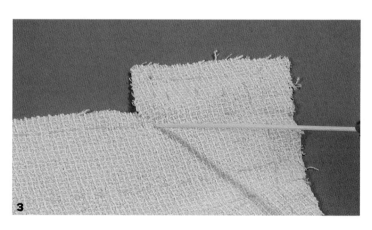

3. Mark the sleeve vent carefully. Be very accurate when marking the corner at the top of the vent. On the front sleeve, carefully mark the matching point for the back sleeve. Mark all notches and construction symbols with tiny running stitches.

4. Cut the hem interfacing. Use large diagonal basting stitches to baste it to the wrong side of the sleeve. Notice that the interfacing does not extend into the hem or seam allowances at the vent opening, and the edges of the interfacing are aligned with the thread tracings.

5. Fold the hem allowance over the interfacing and pin in place. Baste ¼ in. from the folded edge.

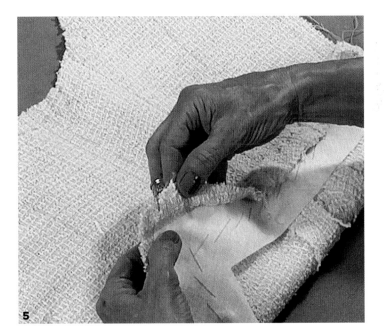

6. At the corner, use a miter to reduce bulk. (See "Mitered Corner" on the facing page for details.) Continue basting ¼ in. from the folded edge of the vent seam allowance. Press.

7. Make a few catchstitches on the seams at the top of the interfacing to hold it in place and prevent it from floating. Permanently sew the hem allowance to the interfacing with catchstitches.

NOTE Contrast thread is used for this sample so you can see it easily. When sewing the garment, use matching thread.

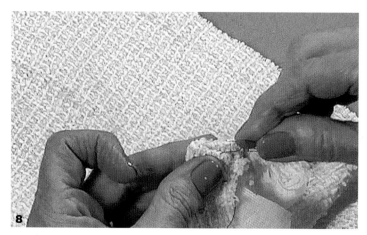

8. At the mitered corners, use fell stitches to hold the miter in place permanently.

NOTE This technique is also used to finish the sleeve hems and the front and neck edges.

MITERED CORNER

This is a technique you will use over and over throughout the construction process.

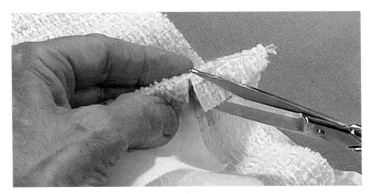

At the corner, clip almost to the marked corner.

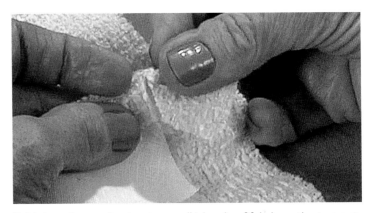

Fold the miter and cut out a small triangle of fabric so the two cut edges butt together.

Use a pin on the seamline to hold the seam allowance in place, and fold the adjacent edge over the pin to form the miter. Pin in place.

ADDING TRIM

This classic jacket is trimmed at the front and neck edges, the sleeve hem, and the sleeve vent. Some Chanel jackets are trimmed at the hem, while others are not. This technique for applying the trim can be used on all edges of the jacket. Once you master the technique, you can use it for any trimmed design that you sew.

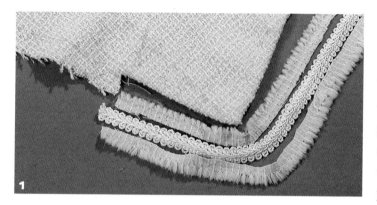

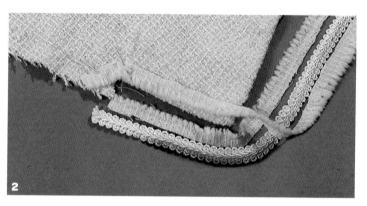

1. The trim for this jacket is composed of three strips of trim: two selvage edges and a piece of gimp or braid. The cut edges of the selvage pieces will be layered and covered with the gimp. Hint: If you don't have enough selvage or don't like the look, you can use a purchased or custom-made piping or lip braid.

2. Begin by pinning the outer piece of selvage along the edge of the vent and hem. This selvage is fringed; it can be placed on the fabric or extend past the edge. At the top of the vent, the trim should extend past the top of the vent and into the seam allowance. Clip the trim at the corner to shape it smoothly.

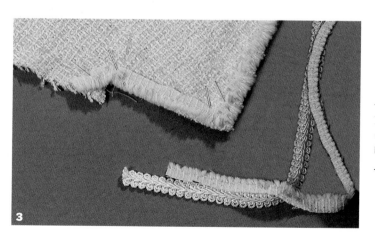

3. At the lower corner, place a pin to hold the trim in place, clip, turn the corner, and pin the trim again.

NOTE Place the second row of selvage in place. Before pinning it to the edge, check the spacing by layering the gimp between the selvages.

4. Pin the second row of selvage in place in the same manner as the first row, extending it past the top of the vent and into the seam allowance. Also clip the corners for neat turns. Sew the selvages in place permanently with short running stitches.

NOTE Contrast thread is used for this sample so you can see it easily. When sewing the garment, use matching thread.

5. Position the gimp between the two rows of selvage and pin in place. Sew it permanently with short running stitches. Occasionally take a back-stitch for added security.

6. The trim is finished except at the ends. Notice that the trim extends into the seam allowance on the front sleeve; it will be hidden inside the seam when the seam is stitched. On the underlap, the raw edges have been wrapped to the underside; they will be covered by the lining.

LINING AND QUILTING

7. The sleeve lining sections have been cut and assembled separately in the same manner as the sleeve. With the wrong sides together, the fabric and lining sleeves were stacked and stitched with four rows of quilting (two on the front sleeve and two on the back sleeve with none on the underarm panel), following the quilting steps in "Where and How to Quilt" on p. 28.

8. At the hem and vent edges, turn under the lining and baste ¼ in. from the edge. Miter the corners as described in "Mitered Corner" on p. 65.

NOTE This technique for finishing the sleeve lining will be used to finish all edges of the jacket.

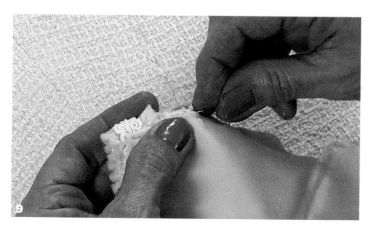

9. Use fell stitches to sew the lining permanently. Notice that the end of the trim on the underlap has been covered by the lining.

BUTTONHOLE MARKING/TEMPLATE

10. Since the buttonholes are not on grain, use a buttonhole template to mark the buttonhole locations. Make a buttonhole template by copying the section of the front pattern with the buttonhole marking. The red marks on the template indicate the actual buttonholes. The vertical foldline indicates one end of the buttonhole; the opposite edge indicates the other end of the buttonhole.

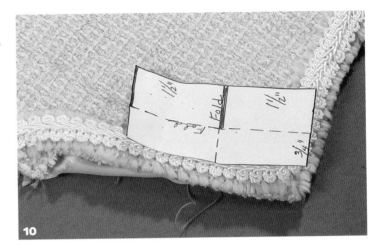

11. Align the template with the edges of the sleeve and anchor it to the fabric with a pin. Fold the template on the vertical foldline and place a pin to mark one end of the button-hole. Fold the template at the bottom button-hole mark and place a pin to mark the buttonhole. Place a pin at the top of the template to mark the top buttonhole. Place a pin on the right edge to mark the remaining end of the buttonhole.

12. Remove the template. Thread-trace along the pins to mark the buttonholes for stitching. Remove the pins. Make handworked buttonholes through all layers. (See Chapter 3 for details on making handworked buttonholes.) Since the vent remains closed when the jacket is worn, the faux bound buttonhole is rarely used on the vent.

STITCHING THE FINAL SEAM

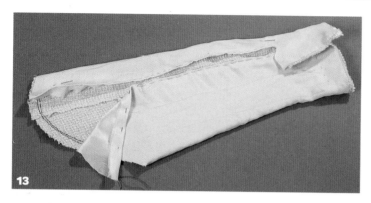

13. With right sides together, hold the lining out of the way to baste, then stitch the fabric sleeve front to the back at the center seam. Remove the basting, press the seam open, and trim the seam as needed at the cap to reduce bulk in the armscye seam. Put two rows of ease basting in the cap where indicated. Follow the steps for "Two Ways to Sew Lining Seams" on p. 44.

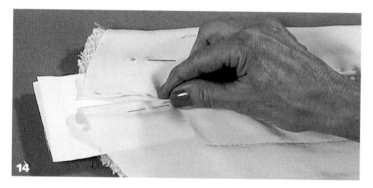

14. Carefully slipstitch the lining seam closed to avoid sewing into the fabric seam. This is especially important at the cap where the sleeve will be joined to the garment.

15. With the lining side out, trim away the fashion fabric seam allowance at the top of the vent. Trim the lining allowance to ¼ in. Fold the trimmed lining seam allowance over the fabric to the right side at the top of the vent. Sew the lining permanently with short running stitches and catchstitches.

16. Pull up the ease basting on the sleeve cap and place the cap on a shoulder stand. Hold the lining out of the way and shrink out the excess fullness to shape the sleeve cap with lots of steam. Press along the stitches with just the tip of the iron. Do not let the point of the iron extend over the seamline more than 1 in. into the sleeve cap.

FINISHING THE VENT

17. With the lining side up, fold the top of the vent over the sleeve front. Use fell stitches to sew it permanently to the lining at the top and for about ½ in. along the edge. (Note: On the companion DVD this technique is shown in Chapter 8, Finishing Details.)

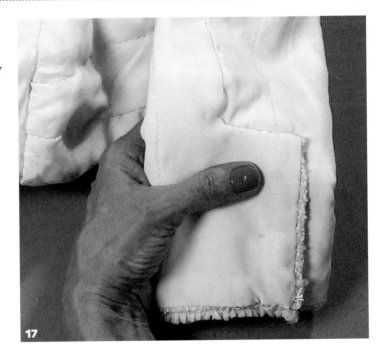

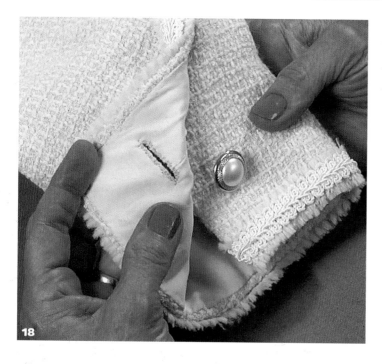

18. The handworked buttonholes have been sewn through the lining. Mark the button locations and sew the buttons in place.

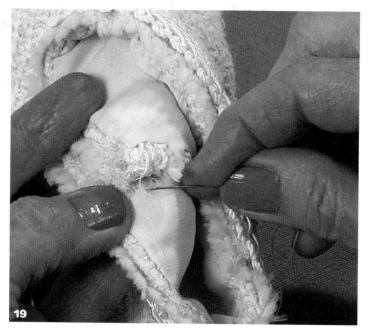

19. Button the vent. Sew a small French tack to hold the underlayer of the vent in place. Do not place it right at the edge, but a little farther up. It isn't necessary to cover it with buttonhole stitches.

TIP Once the sleeves are finished, stuff them with tissue paper so they will hold their shape until you are ready to set them into the jacket.

COUTURE COLLECTION

The impeccably crafted sleeve vent on this Chanel jacket from the mid-1970s features traditional thread buttonholes and buttons with the signature double C logo. This design is very similar to one from the 1960s.

CHAPTER FIVE

Finishing the Edges

The edges of this
velvet jacket were
finished by hand,
and then the piping
was sewn to the
wrong side and the
lining was hand sewn
at the edges.

TECHNIQUES
FOR EDGES

This classic cardigan jacket is lined-to-edge at the front, neckline, and hem. Because most couture jackets have a lining that is quilted to the jacket sections during assembly, the standard home-sewing method for lining a garment to the edge cannot be used: The edges at the hem, neckline, and front are completed with hand stitches using the same basic technique used on the sleeve hem and vent. Once you master the process, it will go very quickly.

Chanel is reported to have said . . . "Clutter is necessary in a room, unnecessary in clothes."

FINISHING THE HEM

As with most couture jackets, this cardigan will have an interfaced hem. The interfacing will give the lower edge body and create a smooth, soft hem. The ideal choice for interfaced hems is wigan, a bias-cut woven fabric made of cotton, sold in precut 2-in.-, 3-in.-, and 4-in.-wide strips. If wigan is not available, you can use a lightweight, crisp woven interfacing.

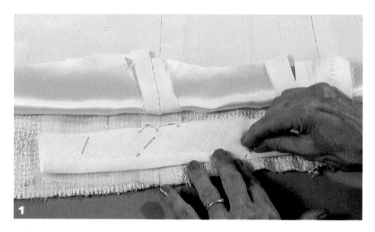

1. Pin the interfacing to the lower edge, overlapping the thread-marked hemline about ½ in. Fold the lower edge of the interfacing at the hemline and pin again.

NOTE Contrast thread is used for these samples so you can see it easily. When sewing the garment, use matching thread.

2. Place catchstitches (red thread) at the top of the interfacing at the jacket seams. Place additional catchstitches between the seams as needed. Work carefully so the stitches won't show on the outside of the garment.

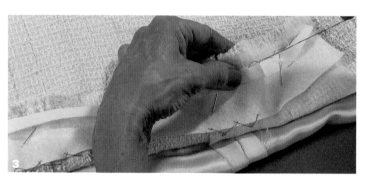

3. Carefully sew the folded edge of the interfacing to the thread-marked hemline with blindstitches so the stitches don't show on the outside of the jacket.

4. Fold the hem allowance over the interfacing and baste in place ¼ in. from the edge (blue thread). Miter the corner at the front edge by clipping into the seam allowance, cutting out a small triangle, butting the cut edges, and folding. (See "Mitered Corner," p. 65, for more details.) Fold the seam allowance to the wrong side at the front edges of the jacket. Finish the hem and front edges with catch-stitches (red thread).

5. Smooth the lining over the hem. Turn under the lining so that it is about ⅜ in. above the finished edge of the jacket. Pin in place. Baste through all layers, ¼ in. from the folded edge of the lining (blue thread). Leave the lining free at the front edge so it can be finished after the trim has been added.

6. Remove the pins and carefully sew the lining hem to the jacket permanently with slipstitches or fell stitches so the stitches don't show on the outside of the garment.

TIP It will be easier to sew the hem if the jacket is turned upside down so you can hold the hem edge in your hand as you sew.

FINISHING THE SHOULDERS

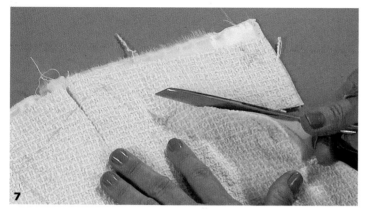

7. Trim away the excess fabric at the neckline and shoulders, leaving 1-in. seam allowances. If the fashion fabric doesn't ravel badly, the seam allowances can be slightly narrower.

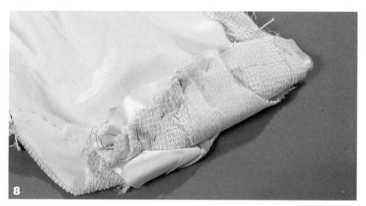

8. Sew a row of ease basting at the back shoulder seam. With right sides together, pin the front shoulder to the back shoulder along the seamline, easing the back to fit the front. Hold the lining out of the way so it is not caught in the pins. Be careful to match the neck point and shoulder point precisely. Baste the seamline from the neck point to $\frac{1}{4}$ in. beyond the shoulder point. Machine-stitch the shoulder seam on the basted line. Remove the basting.

9. Press the stitched seam flat, then place it over a tailor's ham and press it open. Press only the seamline to avoid leaving an impression of the seam allowance edges on the right side of the jacket. Trim the seam allowances at the ends of the seam if needed to reduce bulk.

10. While the shoulder is still on the tailor's ham, you can sew the front and back lining sections together using the lapped method described in "Two Ways to Sew Lining Seams" on p. 44. Smooth the front lining over the shoulder seam and pin in place. Using running stitches and matching thread, sew the front lining to the back shoulder seam allowance, leaving about 2 in. unstitched at the neck; this will be finished later, after the trim is sewn to the neck edge.

11. Fold under the back lining section and pin in place along the seamline. Baste in place, then sew permanently with fell stitches, leaving about 2 in. unstitched at the neck and shoulder.

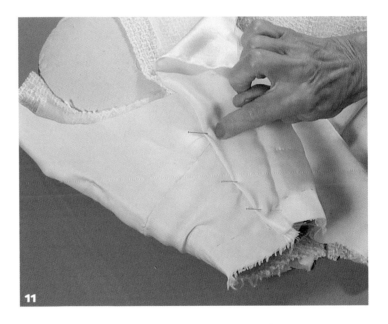

FINISHING THE NECK AND FRONT EDGES

12. Using the thread tracing as a guide, fold the edges to the wrong side of the jacket at the neck edge, mitering the corners at the front edges. (See "Mitered Corner," p. 65, for more details.) Baste in place. Trim the seam allowances. Hold and pin the lining out of the way while the trim is stitched.

13. Sew the trim to the neck and front edges before the lining edge is finished so that all the stitches used to anchor the trim are hidden by the lining. Begin applying the center of the trim to the jacket at the center back neck following the method described in "Adding Trim" on p. 66. Finish the ends of the trim at the hemline by wrapping them over the edge to the wrong side.

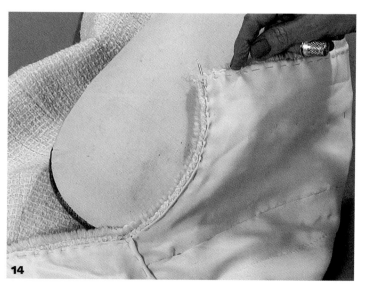

14. To finish the neck and front edges, turn under the lining and pin in place. The lining can extend to the jacket edge or stop ¼ in. to ⅜ in. away. Baste through all layers, then sew permanently with fell stitches. When the neck and front edges have been completed, go back to the shoulder seam and finish the seam with fell stitches.

15. Pickstitches are very tiny back-stitches. They can be placed near the edge of the lining or ¼ in. away to control the lining so that it lies flat and doesn't extend beyond the edge of the jacket. This is especially important if the jacket doesn't have buttons and buttonholes, and is designed to have the front edges meet at the center.

TIP Before beginning, I check to be sure I have enough trim for the neck and the front of each side to avoid piecing. Then I begin at center back and apply the trim to one side, then the other.

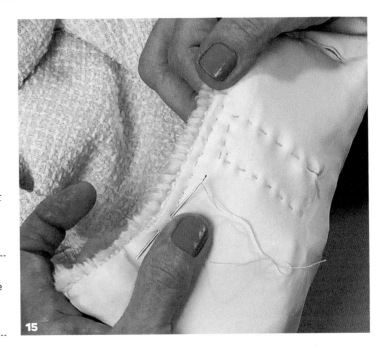

COUTURE COLLECTION

From the late 1970s, this Chanel jacket is fabricated in a printed wool crepe. Pick-stitches were used along the edges of the lining to tame the plain-weave silk fabric so it would lie flat when joined to the wool crepe.

CHAPTER SIX

Setting the Sleeves

Since this coat's center front is the edge of a solid color bar in the fabric pattern, the right and left sleeves were cut individually so they would match the coat front precisely.

HAND-SET SLEEVES

A perfectly set sleeve will fit smoothly into the armscye with the proper amount of ease balanced between the front and back of the shoulder. The easing in the cap is shorter in the front and longer in the back to allow for comfortable forward motion. Hand sewing the sleeve into the armscye affords better control over the easing, offers a little "give," and results in a more professional-looking jacket. Although you may think that hand sewing is not as strong as machine stitching, it can be the opposite when sewn properly.

"One of my favorite Chanel observations . . . 'A sleeve isn't right unless the arm lifts easily.'"

—Claire Shaeffer

HOW TO SET THE SLEEVE

The contours of the sleeve follow those of the arm, so there is a right sleeve and a left sleeve. When setting the sleeve into the armscye, check the notches to avoid inserting the sleeves incorrectly. The front has a single notch and the back has a double notch.

1. Prepare the jacket for the sleeve by basting the lining to the fabric at the armscye along the thread-traced seamline. Next, make a row of back-stitches just inside the seamline on the back armscye for about 3 in., beginning about 2 in. below the shoulder seam. This holds the back armscye a little bit tighter, giving a little fullness to form a small pocket in the shoulder blade area.

2. On the outside, match the center seam of the sleeve to the shoulder seam at the thread-marked seamlines.

3. Reposition the jacket and sleeve so the right sides are together. Pin the sleeve into the armscye, matching the notches. Fold the sleeve lining down to avoid inadvertently catching it in the pins and stitches. Adjust the ease basting in the sleeve cap as needed to match notches. Baste the sleeve into the armscye on the seamline.

4. Sew the sleeve in permanently with backstitches using a double strand of silk thread.

NOTE The advantages of hand sewing the sleeve to the jacket with backstitches are that the seam has a little bit of elasticity and is very comfortable to wear. And it's really easy to sew.

---

5. Trim the armscye seam to ½ in. in the sleeve cap. At the top of the sleeve, the seam is folded into the cap. At the bottom, it will stand up.

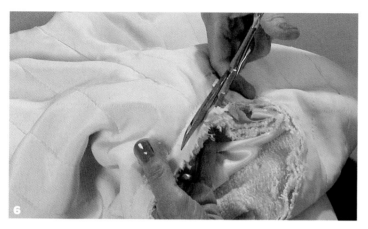

6. Trim the seam at the bottom of the armscye to ¼ in.

7. Press the seam flat to marry the stitches. Do not allow the point of the iron to press into the sleeve cap.

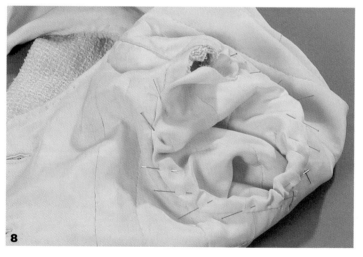

8. Turn under the seam allowance of the sleeve lining and pin to the armscye along the seamline, matching the notches.

9. At the underarm, the lining will go up and over the armscye seam so that the sleeve will drape better.

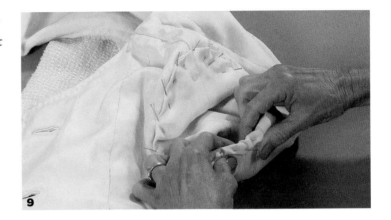

10. Baste the lining seam, easing in any excess fullness as you go. Use fell stitches to sew the lining permanently. Remove the basting threads.

NOTE Don't worry if the lining seam is not eased smoothly; this is an indication that the seam is hand sewn.

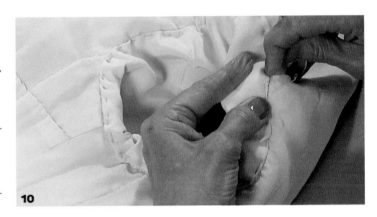

COUTURE COLLECTION

From 1967, this exquisitely made Chanel jacket has perfectly set sleeves. Notice how the fabric pattern is matched at the back of the armscye.

CHAPTER SEVEN

Patch Pocket Techniques

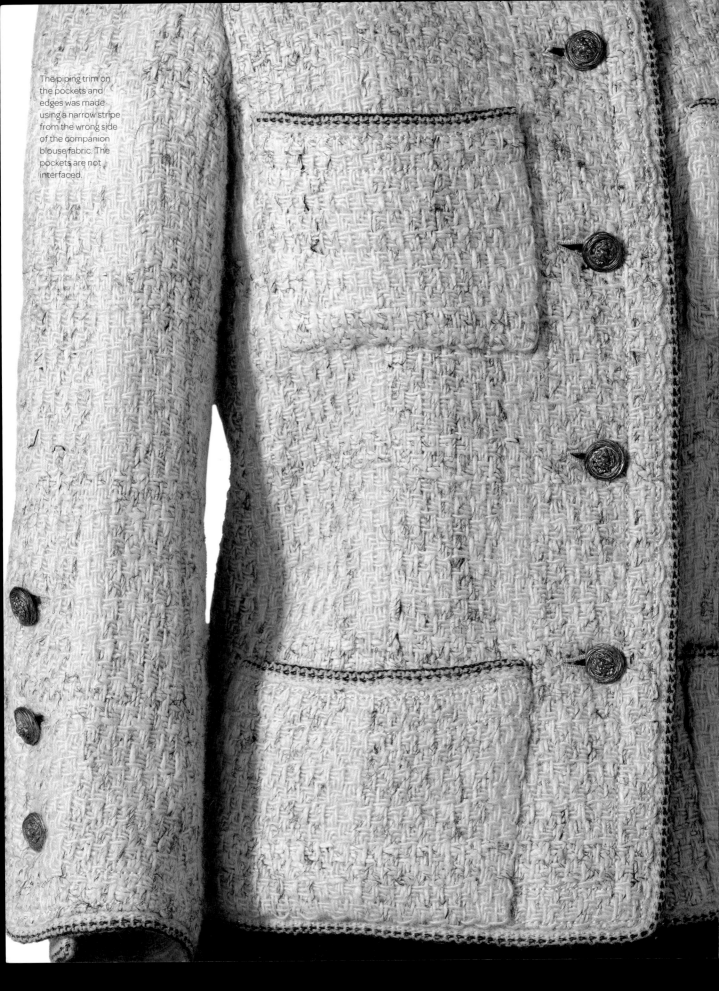

The piping trim on
the pockets and
edges was made
using a narrow stripe
from the wrong side
of the companion
blouse fabric. The
pockets are not
interfaced.

COUTURE PATCH POCKETS

A distinguishing characteristic of Chanel's jackets are the patch pockets. Most garments include two, but some have as many as four. Chanel was extremely creative with pockets—sizes, positions, and trims varied greatly, as did the inclusion of buttons, working buttonholes, and flaps without pockets. This is the time to be imaginative and design pockets that complement your jacket and flatter your shape. In contrast to tailored pockets on couture jackets, these pockets have no interfacing, giving them a softer feeling to match the unconstructed design of the garment.

Pockets are a key feature on many Chanel jackets, and Chanel is reported to have said . . . "Place the pockets accurately for use, never a button without a buttonhole."

HOW TO MAKE A PATCH POCKET

Take the time to make a practice pocket. Pin it to your garment and stand back to look at it. What may seem like a good idea when viewing the pocket alone may be too strong, or too weak, when applied to the jacket. Like many of the Chanel pockets, this pocket is not interfaced, and it will sag. If you don't like this look, add an interfacing.

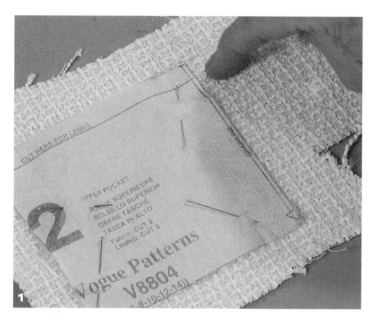

1. Trim away the seam allowances on the pocket pattern. Pin the pattern to a scrap of the fashion fabric with the right side up. Thread-trace around the pattern.

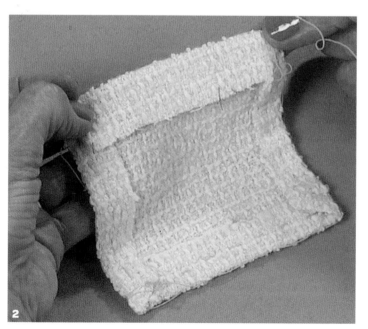

2. Remove the pattern and fold the lower edge of the pocket to the wrong side, using the thread tracing as a guide. Baste ¼ in. from the edge. Then fold the sides under and miter the corners. Last, fold the hem under and miter the corners. (See "Mitered Corner," p. 65, for more details.) Baste ¼ in. from the edges.

3. Carefully sew the seam allowances flat with catchstitches so the stitches don't show on the right side. At the corners, use fell stitches to hold the mitered edges.

NOTE Contrast thread is used for this sample so you can see it easily. When sewing the garment, use matching thread.

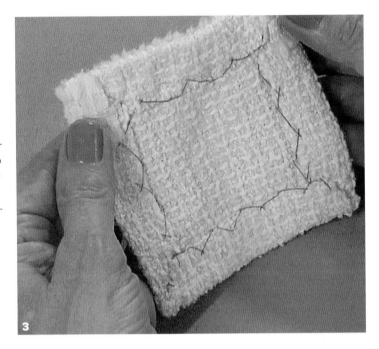

4. Sew the trim to the top edge of the jacket in the same manner as on other areas of the jacket. (See "Adding Trim" on p. 66 for more details.) To finish the ends, wrap them to the wrong side and sew them permanently.

5. Place the finished pocket on a piece of lining fabric, wrong sides together. Hold it in place with a row of diagonal basting in the center of the pocket. Trim away the extra lining fabric, leaving ¼ in. to ⅜ in. at all edges.

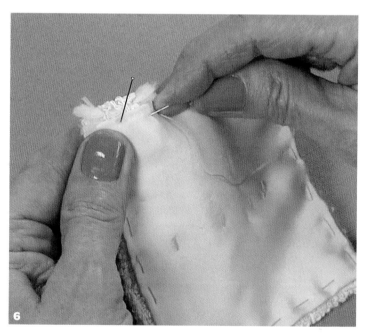

6. Turn under the lining ⅛ in. to ⅜ in. from the edges of the finished pocket. Fold miters at the corners and pin in place. Baste through all layers ¼ in. from the folded edges of the lining. Remove the pins. Use fell stitches to sew the lining permanently.

7. Remove all basting threads. Repeat to make the remaining pockets.

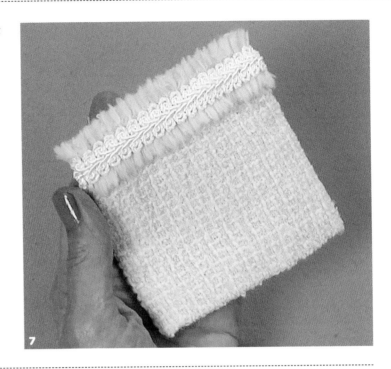

ATTACHING THE POCKETS

8. Place the pockets on the garment in an arrangement to complement your figure. Here, the lower pockets are set at the hemline with the smaller pockets above it, aligned at the edges closest to the opening. Baste the pockets in place about ¼ in. from the pocket edges. (Note: On the companion DVD, this technique is shown in Chapter 8, Finishing Details.)

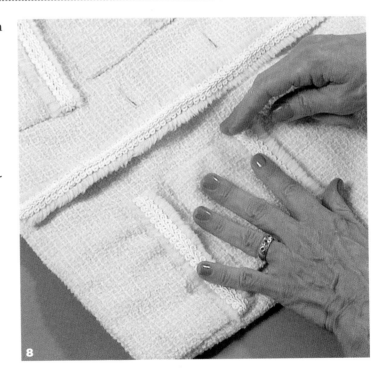

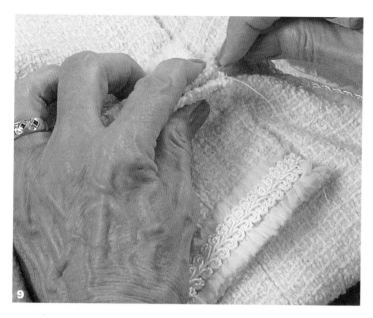

9. Permanently sew the pockets to the jacket with blind stitches. Fasten the thread on the pocket, then take a backstitch. Take a tiny stitch on the jacket without sewing into the lining. Then take a stitch on the pocket just slightly under the folded edge, so the stitches are not visible on the outside. At the end, fasten the thread and hide the end between the fabric layers.

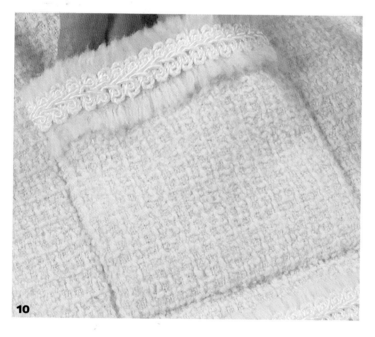

10. Attach all pockets to the jacket following the same procedure. Notice that my cardigan jacket, like many Chanel jackets, has no buttons and buttonholes on the pockets.

COUTURE COLLECTION

This Chanel jacket from the early 1960s has an unusual fabrication. The tweedy wool plaid is lined with double knit, which is then used to make the pocket flaps. A vertical stripe of the jacket fabric is used to trim the neck, front edges, and the welts of the bound buttonholes on the sleeve vents. The pocket flaps feature bound buttonholes with welts made from the jacket fabric.

CHAPTER EIGHT

Finishing Details

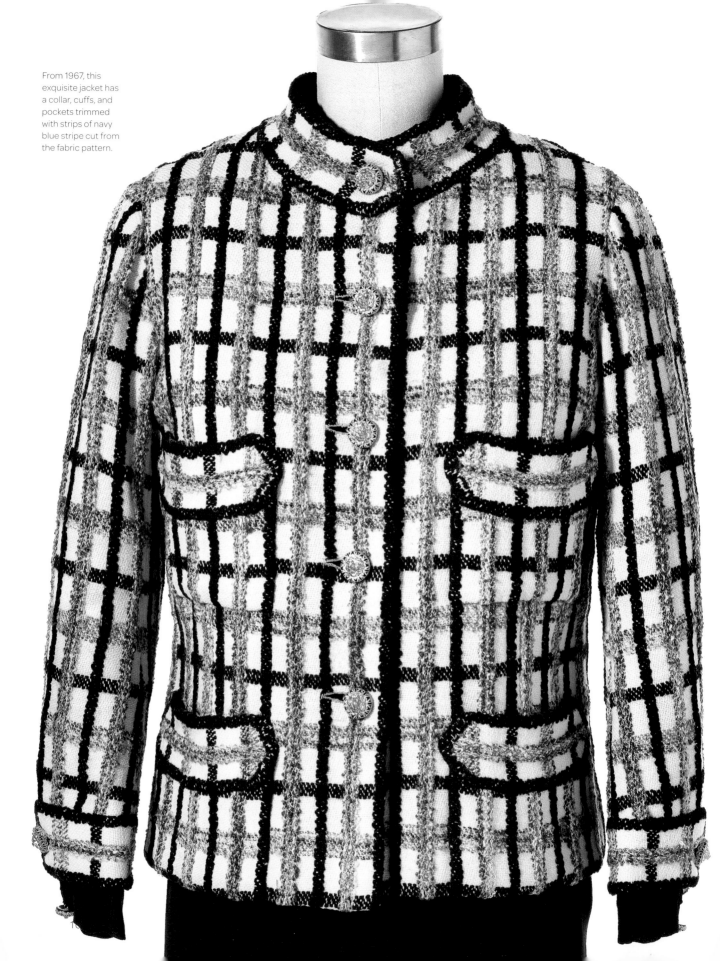

From 1967, this exquisite jacket has a collar, cuffs, and pockets trimmed with strips of navy blue stripe cut from the fabric pattern.

LITTLE DETAILS THAT MAKE A BIG DIFFERENCE

From the simple task of sewing on a button to finishing off the inside of a buttonhole, it's the little details that can take a garment from ordinary to extraordinary. But none of these details is as identified with Chanel's jackets as the chain weight. It is applied to the hemline to counterbalance its lightweight, airy quality. Without the chain, the jacket would catch on other articles of clothing and bunch up when the wearer moves. The weight of the chain brings the jacket back to the proper position on the body. It's a clever—and pretty—design element.

The details shown here may be invisible when the jacket is worn, but they give the wearer the confidence that every aspect of the garment is couture quality, inside and out.

"A favorite Chanel quote: 'You have to breathe and move and sit without being conscious of what you have on.'"

—Claire Shaeffer

HOW TO FINISH THE INSIDE OF THE BUTTONHOLE

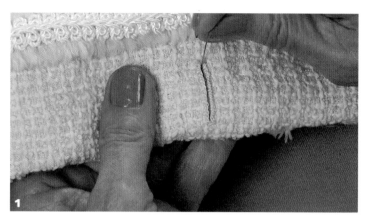

1. Baste around the buttonhole through all layers. This will hold the lining smooth and in position while stitching. From the outside of the garment, mark the ends of the buttonhole with pins.

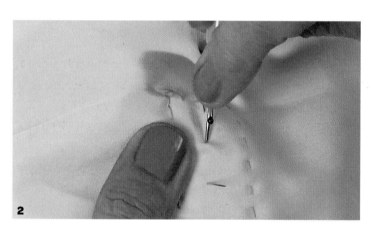

2. On the inside of the garment, the pin points indicate the ends of the buttonhole. Use a seam ripper to start the slit on the lining fabric aligned with the buttonhole. Switch to a small scissors and complete the slit, ending a scant 1/8 in. past the pins that mark the end of the buttonhole.

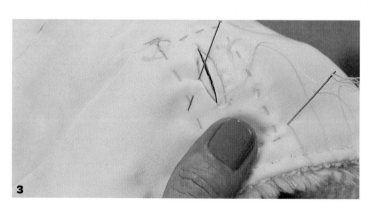

3. Fold under the raw edges of the slit to expose the welts of the buttonhole. Slipstitch the lining permanently. Sew around the buttonhole twice instead of making tiny stitches and sewing once.

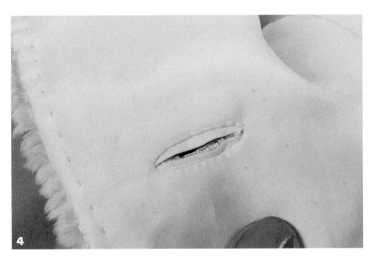

4. Remove the basting threads. Complete all buttonholes in the same manner.

HOW TO SEW ON A BUTTON

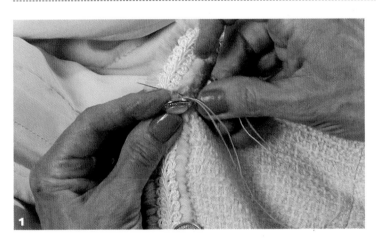

1. Using a single strand of silk buttonhole twist that has been waxed and pressed, fasten the thread to the jacket at the button position. Pass the thread through the shank of the button, which should be oriented so that it is parallel to the buttonhole.

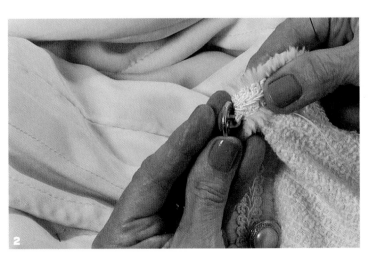

2. Stitch four or five times between the jacket and button. Do not stitch into the lining. Make a knot under the button and bury the thread tails between the fabric layers.

HOW TO ADD SHAPE TO THE JACKET BACK

1. To add some subtle shaping to the jacket, pin several tiny vertical darts in the lining between the center back and side panel. On this sample, they are near the quilting lines. Baste the darts and remove the pins. Carefully sew the darts permanently with fell stitches to avoid catching the fashion fabric.

2. On the outside, there are fabric bubbles caused by the darts. Use lots of steam to shrink the fabric. With the right side up, steam and pat the fabric with your hand. Repeat several times until the fabric matches the shaping of the lining.

COUTURE COLLECTION

Rarely seen inner details of a Chanel jacket from 1964 show the shaped darts added to the lining back—but not the jacket back. The jacket fabric is steamed and shrunk to match the lining shape.

HOW TO ADD A CHAIN WEIGHT

1. There are a variety of chains that can be used at the hemline of a jacket. Where you position the chain in relationship to the hem is also a matter of choice. Don't place it too close to the hemline, or it will pull the hem allowance down and show when worn. I place the chain at least ¼ in. to ⅜ in. from the edge.

2. At the front of the jacket, the chain should not extend past the center front, so that chains don't overlap when the jacket is buttoned. If the jacket has heavy buttons or heavy pockets, place the chain only on the back as a counterbalance. Measure the hemline from the beginning to the end point for the chain, and add 1 in. to 2 in. The chain will be eased toallow for expansion of the fabric. Baste the chain to the jacket in the desired position.

3. Using a single strand of cotton thread and a short needle, sew the chain to the jacket permanently with diagonal stitches placed close to the adjacent link so the thread is hidden. Make a stitch in every other link on one side of the chain, then stitch on the opposite side. Work carefully to keep the stitches from showing on the right side.

CHAPTER NINE

Characteristics of the Couture Cardigan Jacket

The edges of the collar and jacket were first trimmed with a black braid. Then the braid was embroidered with the same chenille yarn used to weave the fabric.

WHAT MAKES CHANEL'S CARDIGAN JACKET DIFFERENT?

Always bold and innovative, Gabrielle (Coco) Chanel introduced an easy-to-wear cardigan jacket suit almost a hundred years ago, but it was not until 1956 that she introduced the iconic design that is more popular than ever today. Why is it so popular? What is it about Chanel's cardigan jacket that has made it the single most important and most copied design in fashion history? A primary reason is that Chanel's jacket is a practical design for women on the go. Unlike many haute couture jackets that are heavily structured, Chanel's softly tailored jackets are simply styled from lightweight fabrics with little or no interfacing. Deceptively simple in appearance, the jackets have a nuanced fit, gracefully engineered to flatter the figure, move with the body, and be as comfortable to wear as a second skin. Practical, yet elegant without obvious effort, the jacket features luxury fabrics, simplicity of design, and attention to detail. It empowers women and provides them with the confidence that the outfit is equally perfect for a society maven, a business executive, or a busy mom. But the most important reasons for its success are that it is flattering for all figure types, and the wearer can be confident that she is well dressed no matter where she goes.

CHARACTERISTICS OF THE CHANEL CARDIGAN JACKET

Often described as "boxy," Chanel's cardigan jackets are inconspicuously shaped to gently follow the curves of the body. Manipulating the fabric with princess seams, quilting, and steam to shrink it where necessary, the iconic silhouette was born. The simplicity of the basic design is the primary reason it can be modified and reinvented by changing the fabric, trims, buttons, pockets, and other design features.

LUXURIOUS FABRICS

Chanel shocked the fashion world when, early in her career, she began making suits from soft jersey knits she had purchased in quantity from textile manufacturer Jean Rodier. Not one to follow the rules, Chanel again made headlines when she began using menswear tweeds for women's suits. Over the years, this timeless classic jacket has most often been made from luxurious wool bouclés and tweeds, but there are many versions in checks, plaids, houndstooth, denim, and stripes. Follow Chanel's lead and think outside the box when making a fabric selection—the jacket can be made in almost any fabric and for any occasion, from sporty to evening. You are limited only by your imagination.

TASTEFUL TRIMMINGS

The iconic jacket of the Comeback years, the period after Chanel returned from exile to reopen her "maison de couture," featured several distinctive elements. The braid trim is perhaps the most recognizable trim. On closer examination of the designer's original garments, one sees that the trims encompassed a vast array of materials. The jackets were trimmed with ornate braids or simple topstitching or left with no trim at all so the fabric spoke for itself. Ribbon, gimp, piping, and fringe were used alone or in combination with other embellishments on Chanel's designs. Trims made of lining or blouse fabrics, contrast materials, or the wrong side of the fashion fabric are also seen. This leads me to wonder if Chanel faced many of the same challenges that home sewers face today with a limited selection of colors and styles to satisfy our tastes. Unleash your creativity and create a trim that is uniquely your own.

This jacket has no braids, fringe, ribbon, or gimp—just wool knit piping dyed to match the wool fabric of the garment.

INNOVATIVE CONSTRUCTION TECHNIQUES

Haute couture construction techniques require a lot of hand sewing, and this jacket is no exception. Couture workrooms use hand sewing because it affords greater control—easing and shaping can be introduced easily during the assembly process. Stretching and shrinking are methods that many couture houses, including Chanel, frequently use to engineer both the fit and the design of the jacket. Chanel is also credited with introducing quilting to high-fashion garments. We can only guess the reasons. In the late 1910s, there was a shortage of heavier fabrics, and quilting was used to provide warmth. During the Comeback years, the reason for the quilting could have been to stabilize and add body to the soft, lightweight fabrics that tended to droop or stretch out of shape easily, or to maintain the shaping that had been carefully added with heat and moisture. By quilting the fashion fabric to the delicate lining fabric, without any filler material, the jackets have structure without stiffness so they maintain the shape and desired comfort level.

This stunning jacket is fabricated in an open-weave fabric and lined with a beige lightweight silk.

DISTINCTIVE DESIGN DETAILS

The iconic Chanel jacket features a variety of distinctive elements: collarless jewel necklines or shaped stand collars, princess seams beginning close to the neck, high armholes to increase mobility, patch pockets, handworked and double buttonholes, working sleeve vents with functional buttonholes, gilt or jewel buttons, and a chain-weighted hem to control the jacket's drape. Very few have shoulder pads. Some details are essential to the jacket's function and comfort level, while others are simply fanciful features. All are quintessential elements of an original Chanel jacket.

Designed before the days of air conditioning, many vintage Chanel suits have sleeveless blouses. Faux cuffs are sewn on or snapped in, to give the illusion of long sleeves.

At first glance, this Davidow jacket looks like a Chanel suit from 1967. Closer examination reveals that there are no buttonholes on the pockets and sleeves, and the plaid in the fabric pattern is not as precisely arranged as it would be on a genuine Chanel.

COPIES AND KNOCKOFFS

The simplicity of the Chanel designs was perfect for inspiration and adaptations. Some were copied precisely using the same fabrics and design features of the originals, while others were adapted so they could be manufactured less expensively. Chanel charged a fee to see the collection, which could be as much as $3,200 (in 1957). This could include the rights to make and sell copies. Using Chanel's *Fiche de Références*—List of Resources—the manufacturer would order the same fabrics, trims, and buttons to produce copies similar to the originals. The most expensive were line-for-line copies, or *répétitions*, custom-made for a specific client in the couture workroom at stores such as I. Magnin, Bergdorf Goodman, and Chez Ninon, who made suits for Jacqueline Kennedy. The workmanship and quality of the *répétitions* were as good as the original Chanels and sometimes cost as much.

"After seeing Yves St. Laurent's first collection, Chanel is reported to have stated that he had excellent taste, remarking, 'The more he copies me, the better taste he displays.'"

—Claire Shaeffer

READY-TO-WEAR LICENSED COPIES

Other American manufacturers used a variety of industry techniques to modify the patterns inconspicuously for mass production of ready-to-wear garments. Even though they used the same fabrics, trims, and buttons as Chanel, their labor costs were much lower, and they could sell the copies for about one-tenth the price of an original Chanel.

Davidow was the most important of these manufacturers; others included Jablow, Harry Frechtel, Seymour Fox, Nan Herzlinger, Burke-Amey, Anne Rubin, Andrew Arkin, Molly for Jack Sarnoff, and the Wallis shops in England. The manufacturers purchased several designs each season to copy for their customers.

When a Chanel original was shown in the editorial pages of *Vogue*, these manufacturers were mentioned. The photo caption would include a list of stores where the copies were sold as well as stores that sold the Chanel original. This made Chanel styles available at every price level. Sadly, relatively few authorized copies of Chanel designs have survived.

Chanel provided a Fiche de Références for copies, which included a sketch for the design, sometimes fabric swatches, and a list of all fabrics, linings, notions, buttons, and trims used to make it. The fabrics are described in detail: the manufacturer, the style number, the color, and, of course, the exact yardage amount for the design.

TELLTALE SIGNS OF A CHANEL COPY

Think you've spotted a real Chanel jacket? At first glance, a suit may look like an authentic couture Chanel, but when examined carefully, there are a few details that will give it away as a copy. Here is what to look for:

- The jacket is not quilted.

- The undercollar is padded with machine stitching instead of hand pad stitching.

- The topstitching on the edges of the collar and front goes through all layers.

- Buttonholes at the center front are bound instead of handworked.

- On pockets with buttons, there are no buttonholes.

- The pockets are machine-topstitched to the garment instead of hand sewn.

- The sleeve vent is not a working vent; there are no buttonholes.

- The three-piece sleeve has a seam in the center, but the undersleeve is wide like a traditional two-piece sleeve.

- The plaid on the sleeves is matched horizontally, but not vertically, to the plaid on the jacket.

- The darts on the back shoulder and at the bust are stitched instead of eased.

- The darts do not match at the shoulders.

On this handsome copy, the horizontal color bars in the fabric pattern match at the armscye, but the vertical color bars are a little too close together.

CHRONOLOGY OF COCO CHANEL
AND THE HOUSE OF CHANEL

Most biographers write that Chanel was less than honest when describing her personal background, and she is even quoted as saying, *"My life didn't please me, so I created my life."* Consequently, research into the early years finds many discrepancies of dates and mysteries of authenticity. In an effort to get to the truth, I relied first on publications of the period such as *Women's Wear Daily*, *Vogue* (American and British), *Harper's Bazaar*, and *Elle*, then on fashion historians Amy de la Haye and Valerie Steele, and lastly on the biographers who knew her. There is no question that Chanel was very successful, but it's quite possible that she popularized designs instead of inventing them. We may never know the true details of her career, and since she outlived her competitors, there was no one to contradict her claims.

1883   August 19, born Gabrielle Bonheur Chanel.

1908   Begins a hat-making career in Paris at 160 boulevard Malesherbes.

1910   Opens a millinery shop, Chanel Modes, in Paris at 21 rue Cambon.

1913   Opens a boutique in Deauville.

Introduces the unlined sport coat, made in Rodier jersey.

1914   Introduces jersey sweaters that slip on over the head.

Introduces the two-piece swimsuit.

1915   Opens her first couture house in Biarritz on the Côte Basque.

A Chanel dress costs 3,000 French francs (approximately $600 in 1915).

1916   Introduces the sport outfit: a coat and dress or coat and skirt.

First published sketch of a Chanel chemise design appears in *Harper's Bazaar*.

Chanel knockoffs sold in New York at Leo D. Greenfield, Inc.

1917   Introduces the jersey jacket, lined with fabric to match dress.

Jacket trimmed (and possibly lined) with plaid to match skirt.

1919   Opens her couture house at 31 rue Cambon, which is still in operation today.

Registers as a *couturière* (dressmaker).

1920   Introduces the quilted coat.

1921   Introduces the collarless, boxy cardigan jacket with skirt.

Launches Chanel No. 5 perfume, developed by the perfume house of Rallet, sold exclusively in her boutiques.

Commissions embroidery from House of Kitmir.

Establishes the iconic double C logo.

1922   Designs costumes for the play *Antigone*, written by Jean Cocteau.

1923   Opens a boutique in Cannes.

Makes famous the short chemise invented by Paul Poiret several years earlier.

1924   Establishes Société Parfums Chanel with Pierre and Paul Wertheimer and Théophile Bader to produce and market Chanel No. 5 and the first line of makeup, featuring lip colors and face powders.

1925   Introduces the jersey Chanel suit.

1926   Popularizes the Little Black Dress that *Vogue* called the "Chanel Ford," even though a designer at Premet had introduced a very successful design in 1922.

Chanel models were copied in all prices from $10 to $250.

Employs 2,000 workers and produces 20,000 originals a year.

1927   Opens a couture house in London; closes Biarritz.

Duke of Westminster puts CC logo on lamppost in Mayfair (London).

1928   Opens Tricot Chanel textiles; incorporates tweeds (traditional menswear fabrics) into her line.

Best & Co. (New York) advertises "Chanel" coats—copies of the popular Chanel chamois coat.

1929   Introduces the unisex style.

Opens boutique on rue Cambon to sell perfume.

1930   Introduces braid trims in her designs.

1931   Goes to Hollywood to design costumes for MGM.

1933   Changes name of Tricot Chanel to Tissus Chanel.

1935   At the peak of her career, employs 4,000 workers, owns five boutiques on rue Cambon, and sells 28,000 suits a year worldwide.

1936   Employees strike and lock Chanel out.

1939   Closes her couture house when France declares war on Germany.

1940   Moves to the Ritz for the duration of World War II.

1946   Moves to Switzerland and lives in self-imposed exile.

1953   Returns to Paris and re-establishes her couture house with 350 employees.

1954   Shows first collection of the Comeback years.

Sells Chanel Couture to Pierre Wertheimer and Les Parfums Chanel.

1955   Creates classic quilted bag with chain named "2.55" for its debut date, February 1955.

1956   Introduces the iconic braid-trimmed Chanel suit.

1957   Receives the Neiman Marcus Award for Distinguished Service in the Field of Fashion.

Creates the legendary two-tone, slingback shoe.

"Chanel look" described as a style by the *New York Times*.

"Chaneleries" used by *Elle* magazine.

1958   *Vogue* magazine coins the term "Chanelisms."

1960   Chanel couture suit costs about $1,000.

"Chanel marrow" used by *Harper's Bazaar*.

1963   Jacqueline Kennedy wears a Chanel *répétition* made by Chez Ninon (New York) to Dallas.

London Sunday Times proposes naming Chanel "First Fashion Immortal."

1969   Davidow copies of Chanel suits cost about $350.

1971   January 10, Coco Chanel dies at the Ritz in Paris.

Gaston Berthelot hired to oversee production of Chanel designs.

1973   Ramon Esparza replaces Berthelot to design couture.

1973   Jean Cazaubon and Yvonne Dudel take over couture designs at Chanel.

1973   Davidow, Inc., an American manufacturer known for its Chanel copies, closes.

1974   Alain Wertheimer (Pierre's grandson) becomes CEO; refuses licensing deals.

1978   Establishment of Chanel Creations, the first Chanel ready-to-wear line; designed by Philippe Guibourgé. Chanel Creations cost about $750; haute couture designs cost about $4,000.

1983   Karl Lagerfeld appointed Artistic Director of Chanel Fashion, designer of all haute couture, ready-to-wear, and accessory collections, a position he still holds today.

A Chanel couture suit costs $6,000 to $15,000+; a ready-to-wear suit costs $3,000.

1997   Acquires Maison Lemarié (feathers).

2002   Acquires Lesage (embroidery), Maison Michel (millinery), Massaro (shoemaking), and Desrues (ornamentation and costume jewelry).

2002   Establishes Paraffection to include all specialty ateliers to preserve the unique expertise of fashion's traditional craftsmen.

2005   Acquires Robert Goossens (gold- and silversmithing) and Massaro (bootmaking).

The Metropolitan Museum of Art in New York honors Chanel with a grand exhibition dedicated to the House of Chanel.

2006   Acquires Guillet (fabric flowers).

2011   Acquires Montex (embroidery).

2012   Chanel haute couture suit costs approx. $50,000; ready-to-wear jacket costs $6,000 to $12,000.

Acquires Barrie (cashmere knitwear) in Hawick, Scotland.

WHEN WAS IT MADE?

My collection primarily encompasses Chanel's Comeback years (1954–1971), what I call the In-Between years (1971–1983), and the Lagerfeld years (1983–present). Dating vintage garments can be a challenge, especially when they are purchased from secondhand stores or online auctions. As a collector, I've spent nearly as much time dating the more than 75 Chanel originals and copies I own, as I have examining their structure and design. Here are some of my discoveries.

Most Chanel suits have a label only on the jacket. Under the label there is a tape—the bolduc—with a number on it. These are reference numbers for the Chanel archives. In addition to the date purchased, the archive records would include the name of the client; the cost of the suit; details about the fabrics, trims, and notions used to make the suit as well as the workroom(s) where it was made; and the number of hours required to make it. With this in mind, I recorded the number of each garment I own, and those I examined in museum collections. Sadly, some had no labels, and on some bolducs the number had faded and was no longer recognizable. Without access to the Chanel archives—which are not open to the public—I found other ways to date my collection.

I looked through old issues of *Vogue*, *Harper's Bazaar*, and *Elle* for photographs of suits. I was first able to precisely date one photographed by *Vogue* in 1960, and so the list began. The earliest suit I have was pictured on the cover of *Elle* in 1957. Slowly my list came together and is shown here.

YEAR	BOLDUC NUMBER
• 1957	05600–05900
• 1960	12000–15200
• 1962	17000
• 1964	23000–24000
• 1965	26000–28000
• 1966	31500
• 1967	33500–34000
• 1969	36000–39687
• 1970	38981
• 1971	41500–43000
• 1972	44000
• 1973	47500
• 1975	53000
• 1983	63750
• 1989	68000
• 1991	69750
• 1992	70000
• 1993	71500
• 1995	73200
• 2003	81500

APPENDIX

TECHNIQUES FOR BUTTONS AND BUTTONHOLES

Button closures are often an intrinsic part of a garment's design. They can serve as decorative accents as well as utilitarian fasteners and can be made from all kinds of materials. Generally, bound buttonholes are used on soft, feminine designs such as afternoon and cocktail dresses. Handworked buttonholes are most often used on fine lingerie, traditional menswear-tailored designs, and skirts.

The garment should always be interfaced properly before buttonholes are made. If it's not, it won't maintain its shape, and the buttonhole won't wear well.

If you have made length adjustments to your garment, you will have to adjust the buttonholes to be evenly spaced between the top and bottom buttonholes.

Always test your buttonhole on a scrap of your fabric with the appropriate underlining and interfacing to discover any problems you might encounter.

MARK THE BUTTONHOLE

1. The size of the buttonhole is determined by the size of the button. Measure the button's diameter and thickness by wrapping a narrow strip of selvage, tape, or ribbon around the button and pinning the edges together.
2. Measure the distance between the strip's fold and the pin, and add 1/8 in. (since buttonholes tend to shrink a little when worked). This is the buttonhole's length.
3. Thread-trace the center front of the garment. This is particularly important for fitting the garment as the center front is pinned together for each fitting.
4. Mark the position and length of your buttonholes with chalk, then thread-trace. Buttonholes should begin 1/8 in. to the side of the center front marking nearest the closing edge.
5. Make a test buttonhole.

HANDWORKED BUTTONHOLES

Sometimes called hand, thread, or embroidered buttonholes, handworked buttonholes are used in couture on a variety of garments, from fine lingerie to tailored coats and suits. Unlike bound buttonholes, handworked buttonholes are cut before they are worked and are generally finished after the rest of the garment is completed. In most workrooms, they are made by a buttonhole specialist.

All of the handworked buttonholes described here require the same careful preparation. Before beginning to sew buttonholes on the garment, perfect your buttonhole stitch and make some sample buttonholes on scraps of your garment fabric. On light- to medium-weight fabrics, use cotton thread or silk machine thread. On heavier fabrics, use silk buttonhole twist.

An easy formula for determining the thread length needed for a buttonhole is to cut the same fraction of a yard as the buttonhole length is of an inch. For example, if the buttonhole is to be 2/3 in. long, cut the thread about 2/3 yd.

Generally, buttonholes are worked with a single strand of thread. Prepare the thread for all the buttonholes before beginning by waxing and pressing it.

PREPARE THE BUTTONHOLE

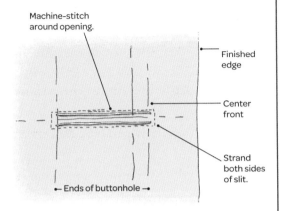

Machine-stitch around opening.

Finished edge

Center front

Strand both sides of slit.

← Ends of buttonhole →

STRAIGHT BUTTONHOLE WITH BAR AND FAN ENDS

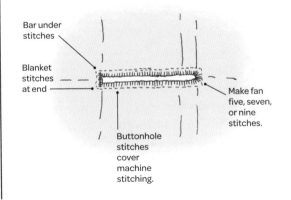

Bar under stitches

Blanket stitches at end

Make fan five, seven, or nine stitches.

Buttonhole stitches cover machine stitching.

1. Thread-trace the buttonhole location and ends.
2. To reduce fraying and prevent the layers from slipping, machine-stitch a rectangle around each buttonhole. Set the stitch length for 20 stitches per inch and sew $1/16$ in. from the thread-traced opening. Begin stitching on one long edge, stitch around the buttonhole, and overlap the beginning three or four stitches.
3. Use a small pair of very sharp scissors or a mat knife to cut the buttonhole opening precisely along a thread in the fabric. To retard fraying when working with loosely woven medium- or heavyweight fabric, seal the edges with beeswax.
4. Overcast the edges of the opening.

NOTE On tailored jackets and coats, stranding—that is, laying in a strand of thread before working the buttonhole stitches—is often used to create a raised texture that attractively defines the buttonhole. Strand the buttonhole immediately after sealing and before overcasting and finishing the edge.

---

5. Using matching thread to strand the buttonhole, anchor it securely at one end $1/16$ in. below the opening. Insert the needle at the other end of the buttonhole the same distance below the opening and take a short stitch between the layers so the needle exits $1/16$ in. above the opening. Repeat this procedure above the opening, so you end where you began. Add a second strand above and below the opening to produce a stronger, more attractive buttonhole; fasten the thread securely at the end.
6. Work either a straight or a keyhole buttonhole by hand.

Straight Buttonhole A straight handworked buttonhole is a simple slit in the fabric with the raw edges finished with buttonhole stitches (see bottom drawing on p. 125). These edges can be finished with a bar at both ends, a fan at both ends, or a bar at one end and a fan at the other. Generally, double-bar buttonholes are used for vertical buttonholes on shirts, while those with fans are used on concealed plackets, blouses, and fine lingerie. Buttonholes with a combination of a fan and bar are used for horizontal buttonholes on bands and cuffs.

1. Begin the buttonhole stitches at the end farthest from the opening, making sure that the purls of the stitches sit on top of the fabric rather than inside the opening.

2. At the end, work a fan with five, seven, or nine stitches, depending on the thread weight and closeness of the stitches. The fan stitches should be evenly spaced, with the center stitch aligned with the opening.

3. Complete the second side of the buttonhole.

4. After the last stitch, slide the needle into the knot of the first stitch to draw the opening together.

5. To make a bar at the end, take three short vertical stitches about 1/8 in. long across the end, pulling the threads taut.

6. Work blanket stitches over the bar, looping the thread toward the buttonhole for strength.

7. To finish, pass the needle to the facing side and secure the thread. Using a diagonal basting stitch, baste the buttonhole closed and press facedown.

8. Remove all the original basting lines.

Keyhole Buttonhole Often used on tailored coats and suits when the fabric layers are thick or bulky, a keyhole, or tailored, buttonhole has one circular end (closest to the garment opening) to allow the shank of a button to be seated in the buttonhole.

KEYHOLE BUTTONHOLE

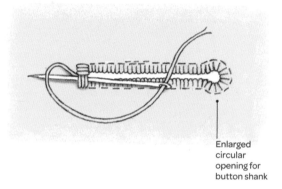

Enlarged circular opening for button shank

1. Insert an awl into the fabric at the end of the buttonhole where the button will sit. Twist to form the circular shape.

2. Machine-stitch around the buttonhole about 1/16 in. from the opening.

3. Cut a straight line for the buttonhole opening and seal the edges with beeswax to prevent fraying. To apply the wax, fold the buttonhole slit lengthwise, with right sides together. Heat the blade of a small paring knife over an iron. Rub the blade over the wax, then rub the slit raw edges with the waxed knife.

4. Work the buttonhole stitches from the straight end to the keyhole. Then work 11 stitches around the keyhole.

5. Work the stitches on the second side and finish the end with a thread bar, as explained in steps 4 through 8 of "Straight Buttonhole" (above left).

1

2

GARMENT INDEX

The garments featured in this book are from my own vintage collection, which has grown to more than 1,700 couture and high-end ready-to-wear designs since I began collecting in the 1970s. They are all Chanel originals from the 1960s, 1970s, and 1980s, except for the Davidow authorized copy. Most were selected because the construction elements included details that are covered in this book, and the techniques could be duplicated by home sewers.

WOOL TWEED

1. Fabricated in a Linton tweed, this classic Chanel jacket from 1967 is trimmed with facings and piping made from the wrong side of an aqua stripe on the blouse fabric. The front has princess seams that begin at the shoulder, but the back has no seams. It has three-piece sleeves with working vents. The collar is cut on the straight grain and shaped into a curve; it was topstitched before the facing was applied. It has double buttonholes at the front opening and traditional thread buttonholes on the sleeve vents. It has a chain at the hem. The quilting rows are placed at the edges of the narrow cream stripes. The bolduc number is 33418.

OPEN-WEAVE STRIPE

2. This stunning jacket is fabricated in a novelty open-weave stripe and underlined with beige silk. The fuchsia tie and facings for the front and collar are cut from the blouse fabric. The solid-color collar and trims were made by stitching tucks in the fabric to remove the beige stripes. It has three-piece sleeves with working vents, a chain weight, double button-holes at the front opening, and traditional thread buttonholes on the sleeve vent. The quilting rows are 3 in. apart. The bolduc number, 39327, indicates that it was made about 1970.

3

4

5

METALLIC BROCADE

3. Fabricated in a silk and metallic brocade, this asymmetrical jacket from the mid-1960s is trimmed with an unusual insertion crocheted with silver metallic yarns and self-fabric tubing woven into the holes. The fly front conceals a simple button/buttonhole closure. The front is shaped with a single vertical dart. It has a chain at the hem and three-piece sleeves set into very high armscyes. Trim is applied to the sleeve, but there is no vent or buttons. There is no quilting and no pocket under the flap. The bolduc number is 30942.

MOHAIR WOOL PLAID, SHORT

4. From the late 1960s, this mohair and wool jacket has no trim. The princess seams are at the outer edge of the vertical gold stripe so the shaping is inconspicuous. The collar is cut on the straight grain and shaped into a curve to fit the neck. It has a chain on the hem, three-piece sleeves with working vents, double buttonholes at the front opening, and traditional thread

buttonholes on the sleeve vents. The buttons are plain. The quilting rows are 2¾ in. apart. The bolduc number is 36958.

MOHAIR WOOL PLAID, LONG

5. This three-quarter-length jacket is fabricated in the same fabric as the short jacket. Both have plain-weave silk linings and plain gold-colored buttons. There is a narrow yoke at the neck edge made by shaping a horizontal stripe into a curved shape to fit the neck edge. The lining extends to the neck, front edges, and hem. It has a chain at the hem, three-piece sleeves with working vents, double buttonholes at the front opening, and traditional thread buttonholes on the sleeve vents. The quilting rows are 2¾ in. apart. The bolduc number is 37237.

6   7   8

WOOL DOUBLE CLOTH

6. Fabricated in black wool double cloth and lined with white plain-weave silk, this jacket from the mid-1970s is very similar to one from the 1960s in a museum collection. It has princess seams on the front and a self-fabric facing at the front edges. The jacket edges, pockets, and flaps are trimmed with a hand sewn fold-over braid. The fabric is not quilted. It has three-piece sleeves with working vents, a chain weight at the hem, and traditional thread buttonholes at the front opening, pocket flaps, and sleeve vents. It has a short French tack under each lapel. The buttons have the double-C logo. The bolduc number is 52067.

WOOL AND CHENILLE

7. Designed by Karl Lagerfeld for Chanel in the late 1990s, this wool and chenille jacket is lined with silk crepe. It has a turn-down collar with a single hook and eye at the neck. The black braid trim is oversewn with red chenille yarn. The three-piece sleeves have work-ing vents on the sleeve back seam with seven buttons and button loops. It has traditional thread buttonholes on the pockets. The jacket is quilted and has a chain weight at the hem. The bolduc number is 71757.

WOOL PLAID

8. From 1967, this jacket is fabricated in wool plaid with green wool facings and trim on the sleeve cuff to match the vest that is part of the suit. It is quilted to a green plain-weave silk lining. A horizontal stripe of the plaid was shaped into a curve for the collar. At the neck and front edges, the jacket and facing were topstitched separately, then hand sewn together with blind stitches. It has a chain weight at the hem, double buttonholes at the front opening, and traditional thread buttonholes on the sleeves. The three-piece sleeves have working vents. The bolduc number is 33162.

9

10

PRINTED WOOL CREPE

9. From the late 1970s, this jacket is fabricated in a printed wool crepe. It has a self-fabric facing. The original plain-weave silk lining had been cut out when I purchased it, leaving small fragments around the quilting rows. The jacket has a leather belt and a novelty stand-up collar with small darts to shape it. All buttonholes are handmade with thread. The three-piece sleeves are trimmed at the wrist with a self-fabric band cut on the straight grain. The tuck seam at the sleeve center was machine-stitched on the sleeve front, then hand sewn to the sleeve back. The jacket has a chain weight at the hem. The bolduc number is 56591.

NOVELTY WOOL PLAID

10. This spring coat from 1971 is fabricated in wool with several novelty fibers and lined with pink silk shantung. The quilting rows are 3 in. apart. The coat has a notched collar and decorative tuck seams on the front and at the center of the three-piece sleeves. It is topstitched with hand-embroidery thread, and unlike most couture designs, the topstiching was stitched through all layers on the collar, lapels, fronts, and sleeve vents. The bolduc number is too faded to read.

11   12   13

VELVET AND SILK

11. This velvet jacket from the mid-1970s is trimmed with a flat satin welt and lip braid. It is lined to the edge with two layers of pink silk—a layer of chiffon over a plain-weave silk. The unquilted jacket has double buttonholes at the front opening and traditional thread buttonholes on the flaps and sleeves. Instead of a chain weight at the hem, it has three gold-colored discs stamped with the Chanel name. The flaps are decorative details without pockets. The bolduc number is 50085.

MOHAIR AND WOOL

12. Photographed in *Vogue* (March 15, 1964), this mohair and wool jacket is trimmed with black yarn whipstitched over the edges. The silk gauze lining is quilted to the shell fabric every 3 in. An exquisite luxury fabric, silk gauze is very fragile; the lining has deteriorated and is badly stained. The jacket has a chain weight, the original black buttons, double buttonholes at the front opening, and traditional thread buttonholes on the sleeves. The three-piece sleeves have working vents; the faux blouse cuffs have been removed. The bolduc number is 24313.

SILK HOUNDSTOOTH

13. Photographed in *Vogue* (March 15, 1960), this jacket is fabricated in a silk suiting with a houndstooth pattern. The lining and trim are navy silk shantung. The bias-cut trim is appliquéd to the neck and front edges, the pockets, and sleeve vents. It has two-piece sleeves with working vents, located at the center of the upper sleeve. Gilt buttons are set into fabric-covered rings. It has traditional thread buttonholes. A few threads remain even though the chain weight has been removed. The bolduc number is 11992.

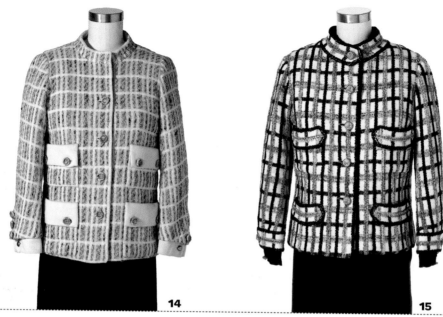

14

15

WOOL TWEED PLAID

14. Fabricated in an unusual wool tweed with a plaid design, this jacket is lined with a cream-colored wool double knit and is quilted horizontally. The double knit is used to trim the pockets and the bound buttonholes at the front opening and sleeve vents, while the jacket fabric is used for the buttonholes on the pockets. The stand collar was cut from a horizontal stripe, then shaped into a curve. The jacket has a chain weight at the hem. The two-piece sleeves have working vents in the center of the upper sleeve as well as faux blouse cuffs. The bolduc number is too faded to read, but the jacket is probably from 1959 or 1960.

WOOL METALLIC PLAID

15. From 1967, this wool plaid quilted jacket is lined to the edge with navy shantung. The navy trim on the collar, sleeve, and pocket cuffs is made from the navy vertical stripe of the jacket fabric. The three-piece sleeves have working vents and traditional thread buttonholes; the front opening has double buttonholes. There is a chain weight at the hem, and faux blouse cuffs are sewn into the jacket sleeves. A photo of the suit is included in the book *Chanel: Collections and Creations* by Daniele Bott. The bolduc number is 33798.

16

17

18

WOOL MOHAIR PLAID

16. This jacket from 1970 is fabricated in a wool and mohair plaid pattern that was then piece dyed. The knit trim was dyed to match. The jacket has been relined to the edge with China silk. The turn-down collar is lined with silk. The jacket has double buttonholes at the front opening and traditional buttonholes on the sleeves. It has flaps with no pockets, a chain weight at the hem, and three-piece sleeves with working vents. The bolduc number is 40642.

WOOL PLAID

17. From 1967, this wool plaid jacket has a notched collar and self-fabric facing trimmed with navy vertical stripes cut from the fabric. The jacket is quilted and lined with white silk. Numerous darts and seams at the edges of the vertical navy color bars shape the jacket attractively. Since it has side vents at the hem, the chain weight is applied to each section separately. It has thread buttonholes at the front opening and sleeve vent. The three-piece sleeves have working vents. The bolduc number is 33214.

DAVIDOW

18. Known for its high-quality Chanel copies, this jacket was manufactured by Davidow and is a copy of a design in the 1967 collection. It has princess seams on the front and back and three-piece sleeves. The jacket is not quilted. The facing was applied to the collar and lapels before they were topstitched. It has bound buttonholes at the opening and buttons without buttonholes on the pockets and sleeve vents. The faux blouse cuffs on the sleeves are sewn into the jacket sleeves. It has a chain weight at the hem.

19

20

CLAIRE'S JACKET A

19. Fabricated in a novelty-weave rayon, the material was selected because of its color so you could easily see the basting threads during construction and the seams when stitched. The fabric is a little softer than I would generally use without an underlining. The trim features rayon gimp set between two fringed selvages. The gimp is readily available and the rayon gimp is softer than polyester, but gimp will add a little crispness to the edges. When using selvages, you rarely have enough to trim the jacket hem and may not want to highlight your hips anyway. The jacket has double buttonholes at the front closure and thread buttonholes on the sleeves. The sleeves are set by hand.

CLAIRE'S JACKET B

20. This jacket was fabricated from the same rayon novelty weave. It was made for me to wear when I accepted the American Sewing Guild Sewing Hall of Fame award. Since I was pressed for time, I eliminated the buttons and buttonholes at the front closure but not the handmade thread buttonholes on the sleeves. The trim is a black insertion with pink middy braid interlaced into the openings. It's set on a narrow ribbon that is barely visible to frame the trim inconspicuously. Both jackets are lined with silk charmeuse. The satin face was used on the lining for this jacket with the dull face on Jacket A because it would film better than the satin.

METRIC EQUIVALENCY CHART

One inch equals approximately 2.54 centimeters. To convert inches to centimeters, multiply the figure in inches by 2.54 and round off to the nearest half centimeter, or use the chart below, whose figures are rounded off (1 centimeter equals 10 millimeters).

⅛ in. = 3 mm	9 in. = 23 cm
¼ in. = 6 mm	10 in. = 25.5 cm
⅜ in. = 1 cm	12 in. = 30.5 cm
½ in. = 1.3 cm	14 in. = 35.5 cm
⅝ in. = 1.5 cm	15 in. = 38 cm
¾ in. = 2 cm	16 in. = 40.5 cm
⅞ in. = 2.2 cm	18 in. = 45.5 cm
1 in. = 2.5 cm	20 in. = 51 cm
2 in. = 5 cm	21 in. = 53.5 cm
3 in. = 7.5 cm	22 in. = 56 cm
4 in. = 10 cm	24 in. = 61 cm
5 in. = 12.5 cm	25 in. = 63.5 cm
6 in. = 15 cm	36 in. = 92 cm
7 in. = 18 cm	45 in. = 114.5 cm
8 in. = 20.5 cm	60 in. = 152 cm

BIBLIOGRAPHY

Abrams, Dennis. *Coco Chanel*. New York: Chelsea House, 2011.

Baillén, Claude. *Chanel Solitaire*. New York: Quadrangle/New York Times Book Co., 1971.

Ballard, Bettina. *In My Fashion*. New York: David McKay Company, Inc., 1960.

Baudot, François. *Chanel*. New York: Assouline, 2003.

Bott, Daniele. *Chanel: Collections and Creations*. London: Thames and Hudson, 2007.

"Chanel Designs Again." *Vogue*, February 15, 1954, 83–84.

"Chanel: Perennial Direction Maker." *American Fabrics*, Fall/Winter 1963, 7.

Chaney, Lisa. *Coco Chanel: An Intimate Life*. New York: Viking, 2011.

Charles-Roux, Edmonde. *Chanel*. Translated by Nancy Amphoux. London: HarperCollins, 1989.

———. *Chanel and Her World*. London: The Vendome Press, 1979.

———. *The World of Coco Chanel*. London: Thames and Hudson, 2005.

Daves, Jessica. *Ready-Made Miracle: The Story of American Fashion for the Millions*. New York: Putnam, 1967.

De la Haye, Amy. *Chanel*. London: V&A Publishing, 2011.

Delay, Claude (née Baillén). *Chanel Solitaire*. Translated by Barbara Bray. London: Collins, 1973.

Fiemeyer, Isabelle. *Intimate Chanel*. Paris: Flammarion SA, 2011.

Galante, Pierre. *Mademoiselle Chanel*. Translated by E. Geist and J. Wood. Chicago: H. Regnery, 1973.

Gidel, Henry. *Coco Chanel*. Paris: Editions Flammarion, 2000.

Haedrich, Marcel. *Coco Chanel: Her Life, Her Secrets*. Translated by C. L. Markmann. London: Robert Hale, 1972.

Hawes, Elizabeth. *Fashion Is Spinach*. New York: Grosset & Dunlap Publishers, 1940.

Holt, Alexia. *Reviewing Chanel: A Catalogue Raisonné and Critical Survey of the Dress Designs by Chanel Published in British and French Vogue 1916–1929*. Glasgow: University of Glasgow, 1997.

Kennett, Frances. *Coco: The Life and Loves of Gabrielle Chanel*. London: Victor Gollancz Ltd., 1989.

Koda, Harold, and Andrew Bolton. *Chanel*. New York: The Metropolitan Museum of Art, 2005.

"Luxury Hidden Away in the Perfection of Detail." *Vogue*, February 15, 1954, 83.

Madsen, Axel. *Coco Chanel: A Biography*. London: Bloomsbury, 1990.

Mazzeo, Tilar J. *The Secret of Chanel No. 5: The Intimate History of the World's Most Famous Perfume*. New York: Harper Collins, 2010.

Morand, Paul. *The Allure of Chanel*. Translated by Euan Cameron. London: Pushkin Press, 2008.

Richards, Melissa. *Chanel: Key Collections*. London: Welcome Rain Publishers, 2000.

Simon, Linda. *Coco Chanel*. London: Reaktion Books, Ltd., 2011.

Steele, Valerie. *Women of Style*. New York: Rizzoli, 1991.

Vaughan, Hal. *Sleeping with the Enemy: Coco Chanel's Secret War*. New York: Alfred A. Knopf, 2011.

Wallach, Janet. *Chanel: Her Style and Her Life*. New York: Nan A. Talese, 1998.

PERIODICALS

Current Biography Yearbook, 1954, 169–171.

Harper's Bazaar, 1954.

Look, October 23, 1962.

New York Times, September 9, 1957, 28.

New York Times, June 12, 1957, 58.

New York Times, November 1, 2012, F9.

The New Yorker, September 28, 1957.

Vogue, 1916–2004.

Vogue, March 15, 1964.

Women's Wear Daily, 1919–1993.

RESOURCES

UNITED STATES

Apple Annie Fabrics
566 Wilbur Ave., Route 103
Swansea, MA 02777
(866) 675-9844
www.appleanniefabrics.com
(fabrics, buttons)

Britex Fabrics
146 Geary St.
San Francisco, CA 94108
(415) 392-2910
www.britexfabrics.com
(fabrics, trims, chain)

David Coffin
1098 Winchuck River Rd.
Brookings, OR 97415
dpcoffin@earthlink.net
(CD The Shaeffer Collection: Chanel)

Eurosteam Evolution Iron
Redfern Enterprises
(877) 387-7770
www.redfern.com
(iron)

Professional Sewing Supplies
2623 Boylston Ave. E.
Seattle, WA 98102
(206) 324-8823
profsewingsupplies@comcast.net
(basting threads)

Sawyer Brook Distinctive Fabrics
P.O. Box 1800
Clinton, MA 01510
(800) 290-2739
www.sawyerbrook.com
(fabrics, buttons)

Superior Threads
87 E. 2580 S.
St. George, UT 84790
(800) 499-1777
www.superiorthreads.com
(silk threads, thread color chart)

Wawak
1059 Powers Rd.
Conklin, NY 13748
(800) 654-2235
www.wawak.com
(wigan)

GREAT BRITAIN

Linton Tweeds Ltd.
Shaddon Mills
Shaddongate
Carlisle, Cumbria
CA2 5TZ
England
44-1228-527-569
www.lintondirect.co.uk

ABOUT THE AUTHOR

CLAIRE B. SHAEFFER is an internationally recognized expert in fashion design and construction techniques for haute couture and high-end ready-to-wear. She is a longtime designer for Vogue Patterns, a frequent contributor to *Threads* magazine, and the author of numerous books. Shaeffer served as Couture Sewing Technique Consultant for the Museum of the City of New York's online exhibit "Worth & Mainbocher." She is the recipient of the Association of Sewing & Design Professional's Lifetime Achievement Award and was recently inducted into the American Sewing Guild Sewing Hall of Fame.

INDEX